中国交通名片丛书

EXPRESSWAYS IN CHINA

中国高速公路

《中国高速公路》编写组

人民交通出版社
北京

深中通道是继港珠澳大桥后粤港澳大湾区建成的又一超大型交通工程，攻克了多项世界级技术难题，创造了多项世界纪录。全体参与者用辛勤付出、坚强毅力，高质量完成了工程任务。这充分说明，中国式现代化是干出来的，伟大事业都成于实干！

——习近平致信祝贺深圳至中山跨江通道建成开通

《人民日报》2024 年 7 月 1 日 01 版

The Shenzhen-Zhongshan Link is another massive transportation project completed in the Guangdong-Hong Kong-Macao Greater Bay Area following the Hong Kong-Zhuhai-Macao Bridge. It managed to overcome numerous global-level technical challenges and set multiple world records. With their diligent efforts and unwavering resolve, all participants successfully completed the project with high quality. This fully illustrates that Chinese modernization can only be achieved through solid work, as all great causes are accomplished through concrete actions.

Xi Jinping sent a letter to congratulate the unveiling of the Shenzhen-Zhongshan Link

People's Daily, July 1, 2024, Page 01

前　言

2021年10月，习近平总书记在联合国第二届全球可持续交通大会开幕式上的主旨讲话中指出，新中国成立以来，几代人逢山开路、遇水架桥，建成了交通大国，正在加快建设交通强国。

今日中国，公路成网，铁路密布，高铁飞驰，巨轮远航，飞机翱翔，邮路畅通，高速铁路、高速公路、城市轨道交通、港口万吨级泊位等规模均跃居世界第一。中国高铁、中国路、中国桥、中国港、中国快递成为亮丽的"中国名片"。

在交通运输波澜壮阔的发展历程中，中国高速公路实现了跨越式发展。1988年，中国大陆实现高速公路零的突破；1999年，高速公路里程突破1万公里；2007年，达到5万公里；2013年，超过10万公里，跃居世界首位；2023年，增至18.36万公里……高速公路的发展，极大缩短了人们之间的时空距离，便利了人民群众的出行，有力支撑了经济社会发展和国家现代化建设。

我们编写出版《中国高速公路》一书，围绕《国家公路网规划（2013年—2030年）》提出的国家高速公路网架构（即7条首都放射线、11条北南纵线、18条东西横线，以及6条地区环线、12条都市圈环线、30条城市绕城环线），以图文并茂的形式集中勾勒、展现中国高速公路发展取得的突出成就。

翻开本书，我们可以领略到大美中国的雄伟壮丽，一条条高速公路跨越江河，穿越山谷，勾勒出一道道迷人的风景线；我们可以触摸到中国经济发展纵横交错的"大动脉"，一条条高速公路为物流高效运转提供了有力支撑，公路两旁一片片区域发展热土相继而成，折射出流动中国的旺盛活力；我们可以感受到神州大地的沧桑巨变，一条条高速公路为乡村振兴、民生改善提供了坚实基础，亿万人民的幸福生活跃然纸上……

奋进新征程，我们要坚持以习近平新时代中国特色社会主义思想为指导，深入学习贯彻习近平总书记关于交通强国的重要论述，继续埋头苦干、担当奉献，再接再厉、再立新功，奋力加快建设交通强国，努力当好中国式现代化的开路先锋，为强国建设、民族复兴作出新的更大贡献。

编者

2024年9月

PREFACE

In October 2021, President Xi Jinping delivered a keynote speech at the opening ceremony of the Second United Nations Global Sustainable Transport Conference, pointing out that since the founding of New China, generation after generation of the Chinese people have worked in the spirit of opening roads through mountains and putting bridges over rivers, and turned China into a country with vast transport infrastructure. Today, Chinese people are redoubling efforts to build China into a country with great transport strength.

China has already built a huge network of highways, railways, ships, airplanes and express delivery routes. China ranks first in the world in terms of the scale of high-speed railways, expressways, urban rail transit, and ports with 10,000-ton berths. China's high-speed railways, roads, bridges, ports and express delivery have become shining "business cards of China".

In the magnificent process of transport development, China's expressways have achieved leapfrog development. In 1988, the first expressway on the Chinese mainland was completed; in 1999, the total mileage of expressways exceeded 10,000 kilometers; in 2007, it reached 50,000 kilometers; in 2013, it exceeded 100,000 kilometers, ranking first in the world; in 2023, the total mileage increased to 183,600 kilometers... The development of expressways has greatly shortened the time and space distance between people, facilitated people's travel, and strongly supported economic and social development as well as national modernization.

We have compiled and published the book "Expressways in China", which focuses on the national expressway network framework proposed in the "National Highway Network Plan (2013-2030)" (namely 7 capital radial lines, 11 north-south vertical lines, 18 east-west horizontal lines, as well as 6 regional ring roads, 12 ring roads in metropolitan circles, and 30 urban ring roads). The book displays the outstanding achievements of China's expressway development in the form of illustrations and texts.

Through reading this book, we can appreciate the magnificent beauty of China. Expressways cross rivers and valleys, outlining fascinating landscapes. We can touch the "arteries" of China's economic development. Expressways provide strong support for the efficient operation of logistics. Hotspots for regional development along both sides of the roads have emerged, reflecting the vibrant vitality of a dynamic China. We can also feel the tremendous changes in the whole country. Expressways lay a solid foundation for rural revitalization and improvement of people's livelihoods, vividly portraying the happy lives of hundreds of millions of people...

As we embark on the new journey, we must adhere to the guidance of Xi Jinping Thought on Socialism with Chinese Characteristics for a New Era, thoroughly study and implement the important discourses of General Secretary Xi Jinping on building China's transport strength, continue to work hard, take on responsibility, stay committed, redouble our efforts, and achieve new successes. We must strive to build China into a country with great transport strength, strive to be the trailblazer in China's modernization drive, and make new and greater contributions to building a powerful country and realizing national rejuvenation.

Editors
September 2024

目 录

首都放射线   001

- G1   北京—哈尔滨高速公路   002
- G2   北京—上海高速公路   006
- G3   北京—台北高速公路   010
- G4   北京—香港澳门高速公路   014
- G5   北京—昆明高速公路   018
- G6   北京—拉萨高速公路   022
- G7   北京—乌鲁木齐高速公路   026

北南纵线   031

- G11   鹤岗—大连高速公路   032
- G15   沈阳—海口高速公路   036
- G25   长春—深圳高速公路   040
- G35   济南—广州高速公路   044
- G45   大庆—广州高速公路   048
- G55   二连浩特—广州高速公路   052
- G59   呼和浩特—北海高速公路   056
- G65   包头—茂名高速公路   060
- G69   银川—百色高速公路   064
- G75   兰州—海口高速公路   068
- G85   银川—昆明高速公路   072

东西横线   077

- G10   绥芬河—满洲里高速公路   078
- G12   珲春—乌兰浩特高速公路   082
- G16   丹东—锡林浩特高速公路   084
- G18   荣成—乌海高速公路   086

- G20   青岛—银川高速公路   090
- G22   青岛—兰州高速公路   092
- G30   连云港—霍尔果斯高速公路   094
- G36   南京—洛阳高速公路   096
- G40   上海—西安高速公路   098
- G42   上海—成都高速公路   102
- G50   上海—重庆高速公路   106
- G56   杭州—瑞丽高速公路   110
- G60   上海—昆明高速公路   114
- G70   福州—银川高速公路   118
- G72   泉州—南宁高速公路   122
- G76   厦门—成都高速公路   124
- G78   汕头—昆明高速公路   128
- G80   广州—昆明高速公路   132

地区环线   135

- G91   辽中地区环线高速公路   136
- G92   杭州湾地区环线高速公路   138
- G93   成渝地区环线高速公路   140
- G94   珠江三角洲地区环线高速公路   142
- G95   首都地区环线高速公路   144
- G98   海南地区环线高速公路   146

都市圈环线   149

城市绕城环线   157

后记   176

CONTENTS

Capital Radial Line — 001

G1	Beijing – Harbin Expressway	002
G2	Beijing – Shanghai Expressway	006
G3	Beijing – Taipei Expressway	010
G4	Beijing – Hong Kong & Macao Expressway	014
G5	Beijing – Kunming Expressway	018
G6	Beijing – Lhasa Expressway	022
G7	Beijing – Urumqi Expressway	026

North–South Vertical Line — 031

G11	Hegang – Dalian Expressway	032
G15	Shenyang – Haikou Expressway	036
G25	Changchun – Shenzhen Expressway	040
G35	Jinan – Guangzhou Expressway	044
G45	Daqing – Guangzhou Expressway	048
G55	Erenhot – Guangzhou Expressway	052
G59	Hohhot – Beihai Expressway	056
G65	Baotou – Maoming Expressway	060
G69	Yinchuan – Baise Expressway	064
G75	Lanzhou – Haikou Expressway	068
G85	Yinchuan – Kunming Expressway	072

East–West Horizontal Line — 077

G10	Suifenhe – Manzhouli Expressway	078
G12	Hunchun – Ulanhot Expressway	082
G16	Dandong – Xilinhot Expressway	084
G18	Rongcheng – Wuhai Expressway	086
G20	Qingdao – Yinchuan Expressway	090
G22	Qingdao – Lanzhou Expressway	092
G30	Lianyungang – Khorgos Expressway	094
G36	Nanjing – Luoyang Expressway	096
G40	Shanghai – Xi'an Expressway	098
G42	Shanghai – Chengdu Expressway	102
G50	Shanghai – Chongqing Expressway	106
G56	Hangzhou – Ruili Expressway	110
G60	Shanghai – Kunming Expressway	114
G70	Fuzhou – Yinchuan Expressway	118
G72	Quanzhou – Nanning Expressway	122
G76	Xiamen – Chengdu Expressway	124
G78	Shantou – Kunming Expressway	128
G80	Guangzhou – Kunming Expressway	132

Regional Ring Road — 135

G91	Ring Expressway in the Central Liaoning Region	136
G92	Ring Expressway in the Hangzhou Bay Area	138
G93	Ring Expressway in the Chengdu – Chongqing Region	140
G94	Ring Expressway in the Pearl River Delta Region	142
G95	Ring Expressway in the Capital Region	144
G98	Ring Expressway in Hainan	146

Ring Road in Metropolitan Circle — 149

Urban Ring Road — 157

Epilogue — 177

首都放射线
CAPITAL RADIAL LINE

| G1 | G2 | G3 | G4 |
| G5 | G6 | G7 |

中国高速公路
EXPRESSWAYS IN CHINA

中国高速公路　　EXPRESSWAYS IN CHINA

北京—哈尔滨高速公路
Beijing-Harbin Expressway

名　　　称：北京—哈尔滨高速公路（京哈高速）
编　　　号：G1
主要控制点：北京、宝坻、唐山、秦皇岛、锦州、沈阳、四平、长春、哈尔滨
联　络　线：G0111（秦皇岛—滨州）、G0112（长春—辽源）
并　行　线：G0121（北京—秦皇岛）、G0122（秦皇岛—沈阳）

Name: Beijing-Harbin Expressway (Jingha Expressway)
Number: G1
Main control points: Beijing, Baodi, Tangshan, Qinhuangdao, Jinzhou, Shenyang, Siping, Changchun, Harbin
Connecting lines: G0111 (Qinhuangdao-Binzhou), G0112 (Changchun-Liaoyuan)
Parallel lines: G0121 (Beijing-Qinhuangdao), G0122 (Qinhuangdao-Shenyang)

▲ G1京哈高速金沟子互通
Jingouzi Interchange on G1 Jingha Expressway

CAPITAL RADIAL LINE 首 都 放 射 线

▲ G1京哈高速北戴河互通
Beidaihe Interchange on G1 Jingha Expressway

003

▲ G1京哈高速辽宁段
Liaoning Section of G1 Jingha Expressway

CAPITAL RADIAL LINE 首 都 放 射 线

▲ G1京哈高速天津段
Tianjin Section of G1 Jingha Expressway

▲ G1京哈高速兴城服务区
Xingcheng Service Area along G1 Jingha Expressway

　　G1京哈高速是国家高速公路网7条首都放射线中的首条放射线，是连接北京、河北、天津、辽宁、吉林、黑龙江的重要省际大通道；是连接京津冀与东北地区，沟通华北与东北的公路运输大动脉。

G1 Jingha Expressway is the first radial line of the 7 capital radial lines in the national expressway network, and it is an important inter-provincial corridor connecting Beijing, Hebei, Tianjin, Liaoning, Jilin and Heilongjiang. It is a major artery of highway transportation connecting North and Northeast China.

G2 北京—上海高速公路
Beijing-Shanghai Expressway

▲ G2 京沪高速竹园互通
Zhuyuan Interchange on G2 Jinghu Expressway

CAPITAL RADIAL LINE　　首都放射线

▲ G2京沪高速丁伙互通
Dinghuo Interchange on G2 Jinghu Expressway

▲ G2京沪高速江阴大桥
Jiangyin Bridge on G2 Jinghu Expressway

▲ G2京沪高速舫河大桥
Benghe River Bridge on G2 Jinghu Expressway

名　　称：	北京—上海高速公路（京沪高速）
编　　号：	G2
主要控制点：	北京、天津、沧州、济南、莱芜、临沂、淮安、江都、江阴、无锡、苏州、上海
联 络 线：	G0211（天津—石家庄）、G0212（武清—滨海新区）

Name: Beijing-Shanghai Expressway (Jinghu Expressway)
Number: G2
Main control points: Beijing, Tianjin, Cangzhou, Jinan, Laiwu, Linyi, Huai'an, Jiangdu, Jiangyin, Wuxi, Suzhou, Shanghai
Connecting lines: G0211 (Tianjin-Shijiazhuang), G0212 (Wuqing-Binhai New Area)

G2京沪高速是国家高速公路网7条首都放射线中的第二条放射线，是连接北京、河北、天津、山东、江苏、上海的重要省际大通道，是沟通环渤海地区和长江三角洲的主通道，在华北与华东之间形成了一条经济、便捷、快速的公路运输大通道，对促进沿线经济发展具有重要意义。

CAPITAL RADIAL LINE　　首 都 放 射 线

▲ G2京沪高速正谊服务区
Zhengyi Service Area along G2 Jinghu Expressway

G2 Jinghu Expressway is the second radial line of the 7 capital radial lines in the national expressway network, and it is an important inter-provincial corridor connecting Beijing, Hebei, Tianjin, Shandong, Jiangsu and Shanghai. It is the main corridor connecting the Bohai Economic Circle and the Yangtze River Delta, and it has formed an economic, convenient and rapid highway transportation corridor between North and East China, which has an important significance in promoting the economic development along the route.

中国高速公路 · EXPRESSWAYS IN CHINA

G3 北京—台北高速公路
Beijing-Taipei Expressway

▲ G3京台高速渊底枢纽
Yuandi Junction on G3 Jingtai Expressway

名　　称：北京—台北高速公路（京台高速）
编　　号：G3
主要控制点：北京、廊坊、沧州、德州、济南、泰安、曲阜、徐州、蚌埠、合肥、铜陵、黄山、
　　　　　　衢州、建瓯、福州、台北
联 络 线：G0311（济南—聊城）
并 行 线：G0321（德州—上饶）、G0322（北京—德州）、G0323（济宁—合肥）

Name: Beijing-Taipei Expressway (Jingtai Expressway)
Number: G3
Main control points: Beijing, Langfang, Cangzhou, Dezhou, Jinan, Tai'an, Qufu, Xuzhou, Bengbu, Hefei, Tongling, Huangshan, Quzhou, Jian'ou, Fuzhou, Taipei
Connecting line: G0311 (Jinan-Liaocheng)
Parallel lines: G0321 (Dezhou-Shangrao), G0322 (Beijing-Dezhou), G0323 (Jining-Hefei)

CAPITAL RADIAL LINE　　首 都 放 射 线

▲ G3京台高速安徽段
Anhui Section of G3 Jingtai Expressway

▲ G3京台高速平潭海峡公铁两用大桥
Pingtan Strait Road-Rail Bridge on G3 Jingtai Expressway

G3 京台高速是国家高速公路网 7 条首都放射线中的第三条放射线。G3 京台高速的建设对于加强两岸联系、促进两岸经济发展意义重大。

◀ G3京台高速五里枢纽
Wuli Junction on G3 Jingtai Expressway

CAPITAL RADIAL LINE 首 都 放 射 线

G3 Jingtai Expressway is the third radial line of the 7 capital radial lines in the national expressway network. The construction of the G3 Jingtai Expressway is of great significance for strengthening cross-Strait ties and promoting economic development on both sides of the Taiwan Strait.

▶ G3京台高速建州服务区
Jianzhou Service Area along G3 Jingtai Expressway

中国高速公路　　　　　　　　　EXPRESSWAYS IN CHINA

G4 北京—香港澳门高速公路
Beijing-Hong Kong-Macao Expressway

CAPITAL RADIAL LINE　　首 都 放 射 线

▲ G4京港澳高速卫辉望京楼站互通
Interchange of Weihui Wangjinglou Station on G4 Jinggang'ao Expressway

名　　　称：北京—香港澳门高速公路（京港澳高速）
编　　　号：G4
主要控制点：北京、保定、石家庄、邯郸、新乡、郑州、漯河、信阳、武汉、咸宁、岳阳、长沙、株洲、衡阳、郴州、韶关、广州、深圳、香港（口岸）
联 络 线：G0411（安阳—长治）、G0412（深圳—南宁）、G0413（新乐—忻州）
并 行 线：G0421（许昌—广州）、G0422（武汉—深圳）、G0423（乐昌—广州）、G0424（北京—武汉）、G0425（广州—澳门）

Name: Beijing-Hong Kong-Macao Expressway (Jinggang'ao Expressway)
Number: G4
Main control points: Beijing, Baoding, Shijiazhuang, Handan, Xinxiang, Zhengzhou, Luohe, Xinyang, Wuhan, Xianning, Yueyang, Changsha, Zhuzhou, Hengyang, Chenzhou, Shaoguan, Guangzhou, Shenzhen, Hong Kong (checkpoint)
Connecting lines: G0411 (Anyang-Changzhi), G0412 (Shenzhen-Nanning), G0413 (Xinle-Xinzhou)
Parallel lines: G0421 (Xuchang-Guangzhou), G0422 (Wuhan-Shenzhen), G0423 (Lechang-Guangzhou), G0424 (Beijing-Wuhan), G0425 (Guangzhou-Macao)

◀ G4京港澳高速梨园桥互通
Liyuanqiao Interchange on G4 Jinggang'ao Expressway

▲ G4京港澳高速刘江黄河大桥
Liujiang Yellow River Bridge on G4 Jinggang'ao Expressway

▲ G4京港澳高速军山长江大桥
Junshan Yangtze River Bridge on G4 Jinggang'ao Expressway

CAPITAL RADIAL LINE 首都放射线

G4 京港澳高速是国家高速公路网 7 条首都放射线中的第四条放射线，是华北、华中、华南联结首都的主动脉，沟通京津冀地区、中原地区、江汉平原、湘中平原、珠江三角洲等城镇密集区，连通港澳，是我国最繁忙的交通通道之一。

G4 Jinggang'ao Expressway is the fourth radial line of the 7 capital radial lines in the national expressway network. It is a principal artery connecting Beijing with North China, Central China and South China, and communicating with the dense urban areas of Beijing-Tianjin-Hebei region, the Central Plains, the Jianghan Plain, the Central Plain of Hunan province, and the Pearl River Delta, connecting with Hong Kong and Macao. It is one of the busiest transportation corridors in China.

▲ G4京港澳高速耒阳服务区
Leiyang Service Area along G4 Jinggang'ao Expressway

中国高速公路 — EXPRESSWAYS IN CHINA

北京—昆明高速公路
Beijing-Kunming Expressway

名　　　称：北京—昆明高速公路（京昆高速）
编　　　号：G5
主要控制点：北京、保定、石家庄、盂县、太原、临汾、西安、汉中、广元、绵阳、成都、雅安、西昌、攀枝花、昆明
联　络　线：G0511（德阳—都江堰）、G0512（成都—乐山）、G0513（平遥—洛阳）

Name: Beijing-Kunming Expressway (Jingkun Expressway)
Number: G5
Main control points: Beijing, Baoding, Shijiazhuang, Yuxian, Taiyuan, Linfen, Xi'an, Hanzhong, Guangyuan, Mianyang, Chengdu, Ya'an, Xichang, Panzhihua, Kunming
Connecting lines: G0511 (Deyang-Dujiangyan), G0512 (Chengdu-Leshan), G0513 (Pingyao-Luoyang)

　　G5 京昆高速是国家高速公路网 7 条首都放射线中的第五条放射线，是连接北京、河北、山西、陕西、四川、云南的重要省际大通道，是首都沟通西北与西南地区的交通大动脉，是山西中部、陕西北部、宁夏北部物资运输出港最便捷的路径，对加快沿线地区工业及农副产品的流通、推进资源优化配置、带动旅游业发展具有重要作用和意义，将给沿线地区经济社会发展增加新引擎。

G5 Jingkun Expressway is the fifth radial line of the 7 capital radial lines in the national expressway network, and it is an important inter-provincial corridor connecting Beijing, Hebei, Shanxi, Shaanxi, Sichuan and Yunnan. It is the most convenient route for transportation of materials out of central Shanxi, northern Shaanxi, and northern Ningxia. It has an important significance in accelerating the circulation of industry and agricultural and sideline products in the areas along the route, promoting the optimal allocation of resources, and driving the development of tourism, and will add a new engine to the economic and social development of the areas along the route.

▲ G5京昆高速干海子特大桥
Ganhaizi Grand Bridge on G5 Jingkun Expressway

CAPITAL RADIAL LINE 首都放射线

▲ G5京昆高速对岩互通
Duiyan Interchange on G5 Jingkun Expressway

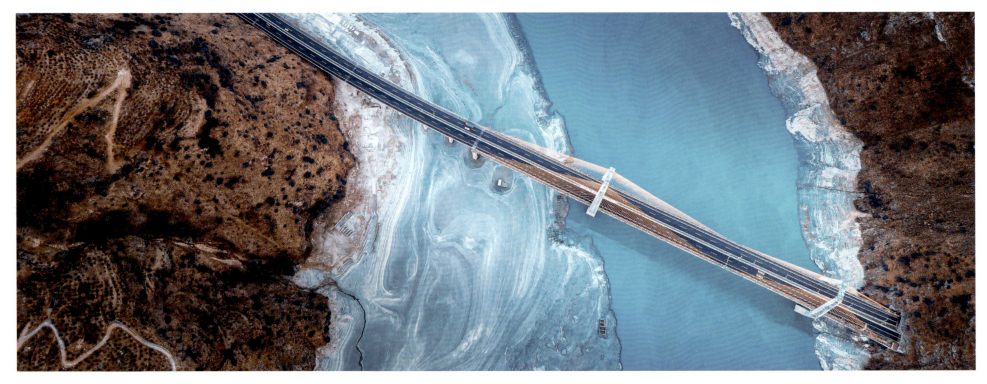

▲ G5京昆高速观音岩大渡河大桥
Guanyinyan Dadu River Bridge on G5 Jingkun Expressway

▲ G5京昆高速腊八斤特大桥
Labajin Grand Bridge on G5 Jingkun Expressway

▲ G5京昆高速金鸡关收费站
Jinjiguan Toll Station on G5 Jingkun Expressway

CAPITAL RADIAL LINE　　　　　　首 都 放 射 线

▲ G5京昆高速荥经服务区
Yingjing Service Area along G5 Jingkun Expressway

北京—拉萨高速公路
Beijing-Lhasa Expressway

▲ G6京藏高速东倾沟互通
Dongqinggou Interchange on G6 Jingzang Expressway

名　　称：	北京—拉萨高速公路（京藏高速）
编　　号：	G6
主要控制点：	北京、张家口、集宁、呼和浩特、包头、临河、乌海、银川、中宁、白银、兰州、西宁、格尔木、拉萨
联　络　线：	G0611（张掖—汶川）、G0612（西宁—和田）、G0613（西宁—丽江）、G0615（德令哈—康定）、G0616（乌拉特前旗—甘其毛都）

Name: Beijing-Lhasa Expressway (Jingzang Expressway)
Number: G6
Main control points: Beijing, Zhangjiakou, Jining, Hohhot, Baotou, Linhe, Wuhai, Yinchuan, Zhongning, Baiyin, Lanzhou, Xining, Golmud, Lhasa
Connecting lines: G0611 (Zhangye-Wenchuan), G0612 (Xining-Hetian), G0613 (Xining-Lijiang), G0615 (Delingha-Kangding), G0616 (Urad Front Banner -Ganqimaodu)

▲ G6京藏高速吴忠黄河大桥
Wuzhong Yellow River Bridge on G6 Jingzang Expressway

G6京藏高速是国家高速公路网7条首都放射线中的第六条放射线，是连接北京、河北、内蒙古、宁夏、甘肃、青海、西藏的重要省际大通道，是沟通首都和西北地区及西藏的重要通道。

▶ G6京藏高速青海段
Qinghai Section of G6 Jingzang Expressway

▲ G109国道和G6京藏高速
G109 National Highway and G6 Jingzang Expressway

CAPITAL RADIAL LINE 首都放射线

G6 Jingzang Expressway is the sixth radial line of the 7 capital radial lines in the national expressway network, and it is an important inter-provincial corridor connecting Beijing, Hebei, Inner Mongolia, Ningxia, Gansu, Qinghai and Xizang. It is an important highway corridor connecting Beijing with Northwest China and Xizang.

◀ G6京藏高速甘肃段
Gansu Section of G6 Jingzang Expressway

▲ G0613西宁—丽江高速虎跳峡金沙江大桥
Jinsha River Bridge through Tiger Leaping Gorge on G0613 Xining-Lijiang Expressway

▲ G6京藏高速八达岭段高架桥
Badaling Viaduct on G6 Jingzang Expressway

中国高速公路　　　　　　　　　　　　　　　　　　EXPRESSWAYS IN CHINA

北京—乌鲁木齐高速公路
Beijing-Urumqi Expressway

名　　称：北京—乌鲁木齐高速公路（京新高速）
编　　号：G7
主要控制点：北京、张家口、集宁、呼和浩特、临河、额济纳旗、哈密（梧桐大泉）、
　　　　　伊吾、巴里坤、奇台、阜康、乌鲁木齐
联 络 线：G0711（乌鲁木齐—若羌）、G0712（额济纳旗—策克）

Name: Beijing-Urumqi Expressway (Jingxin Expressway)
Number: G7
Main control points: Beijing, Zhangjiakou, Jining, Hohhot, Linhe, Ejina Banner, Hami (Wutong Daquan), Yiwu, Balikun, Qitai, Fukang, Urumqi
Connecting lines: G0711 (Urumqi-Ruoqiang), G0712 (Ejina Banner-Ceke)

　　G7 京新高速是国家高速公路网 7 条首都放射线中的第七条放射线，连接北京、河北、山西、内蒙古、甘肃、新疆，横贯东北、华北、西北。G7 京新高速是西北新疆和河西走廊连接首都北京、华北、东北最为便捷的公路通道。

▶ G7京新高速甘泉堡枢纽立交
　 Ganquanpu Junction Interchange on G7 Jingxin Expressway

CAPITAL RADIAL LINE 首 都 放 射 线

G7 Jingxin Expressway is the seventh radial line of the 7 capital radial lines in the national expressway network, connecting Beijing, Hebei, Shanxi, Inner Mongolia, Gansu and Xinjiang, spreading across Northeast China, North China and Northwest China. G7 Jingxin Expressway is the most convenient highway corridor connecting northwest Xinjiang and Hexi Corridor to Beijing, North China and Northeast China.

▼ G7京新高速甘肃段
Gansu Section of G7 Jingxin Expressway

▲ G7京新高速巴里坤木垒无人区高架桥
Viaduct in Balikun Mulei No Man's Land on G7 Jingxin Expressway

▲ G7京新高速北京段
Beijing Section of G7 Jingxin Expressway

▲ G7京新高速新疆段
Xinjiang Section of G7 Jingxin Expressway

CAPITAL RADIAL LINE 首都放射线

▲ G7京新高速黑鹰山服务区
Heiyingshan Service Area along G7 Jingxin Expressway

北南纵线
NORTH−SOUTH VERTICAL LINE

G11	G15	G25	G35
G45	G55	G59	G65
G69	G75	G85	

中国高速公路
EXPRESSWAYS IN CHINA

鹤岗—大连高速公路
Hegang–Dalian Expressway

▲ G11鹤大高速吉林段
Jilin Section of G11 Heda Expressway

NORTH-SOUTH VERTICAL LINE 北 南 纵 线

▲ G1113丹东—阜新高速辽宁段
Liaoning Section of G1113 Dandong-Fuxin Expressway

名　　　称：鹤岗—大连高速公路（鹤大高速）
编　　　号：G11
主要控制点：鹤岗、佳木斯、鸡西、牡丹江、敦化、通化、丹东、大连
联　络　线：G1111（鹤岗—哈尔滨）、G1112（集安—双辽）、G1113（丹东—阜新）、G1115（鸡西—建三江）、G1116（伊春—北安）、G1117（绥化—北安）、G1118（抚松—长白）、G1119（白山—临江）、G1131（牡丹江—延吉）

Name: Hegang-Dalian Expressway (Heda Expressway)
Number: G11
Main control points: Hegang, Jiamusi, Jixi, Mudanjiang, Dunhua, Tonghua, Dandong, Dalian
Connecting lines: G1111 (Hegang-Harbin), G1112 (Ji'an-Shuangliao), G1113 (Dandong-Fuxin), G1115 (Jixi-Jiansanjiang), G1116 (Yichun-Bei'an), G1117 (Suihua-Bei'an), G1118 (Fusong-Changbai), G1119 (Baishan-Linjiang), G1131 (Mudanjiang-Yanji)

▲ G11鹤大高速西湖岫大桥
Xihuxiu Bridge on G11 Heda Expressway

▲ G11鹤大高速辽宁段
Liaoning Section of G11 Heda Expressway

NORTH-SOUTH VERTICAL LINE 北 南 纵 线

G11鹤大高速是国家高速公路网11条北南纵线中的第一纵，是连接黑龙江、吉林、辽宁的重要省际大通道。G11鹤大高速纵贯黑、吉、辽三省东部地区，是黑龙江和吉林两省东部地区通过辽宁进关达海的一条南北快速公路通道，也是环渤海都市圈向东北腹地辐射的重要经济通道。

G11 Heda Expressway is the first vertical line of the 11 north-south vertical lines in the national expressway network, and it is an important inter-provincial corridor connecting Heilongjiang, Jilin and Liaoning. G11 Heda Expressway runs through the eastern part of Heilongjiang, Jilin and Liaoning provinces, and it is an important economic corridor for the Bohai Rim to radiate into the northeastern hinterland.

◀ G11鹤大高速黑沟特大桥
Heigou Grand Bridge on G11 Heda Expressway

▲ G11鹤大高速大泉眼隧道
Daquanyan Tunnel on G11 Heda Expressway

中国高速公路 | EXPRESSWAYS IN CHINA

沈阳—海口高速公路
Shenyang-Haikou Expressway

▼ G15沈海高速大昌立交
Dachang Interchange on G15 Shenhai Expressway

NORTH-SOUTH VERTICAL LINE 北南纵线

名　　称：沈阳—海口高速公路（沈海高速）
编　　号：G15
主要控制点：沈阳、辽阳、鞍山、海城、大连、烟台、青岛、日照、连云港、盐城、南通、常熟、太仓、上海、宁波、台州、温州、宁德、福州、泉州、厦门、汕头、汕尾、深圳、广州、佛山、开平、阳江、茂名、湛江、海口
联　络　线：G1511（日照—兰考）、G1512（宁波—金华）、G1513（温州—丽水）、G1514（宁德—上饶）、G1515（盐城—靖江）、G1516（盐城—洛阳）、G1517（莆田—炎陵）、G1518（盐城—蚌埠）、G1519（南通—如东）、G1531（上海—慈溪）、G1532（泉州—梅州）、G1533（泉州—金门）、G1534（厦门—金门）、G1535（潮州—南昌）、G1536（东莞—广州）
并　行　线：G1521（常熟—嘉善）、G1522（常熟—台州）、G1523（宁波—东莞）

Name: Shenyang-Haikou Expressway (Shenhai Expressway)
Number: G15
Main control points: Shenyang, Liaoyang, Anshan, Haicheng, Dalian, Yantai, Qingdao, Rizhao, Lianyungang, Yancheng, Nantong, Changshu, Taicang, Shanghai, Ningbo, Taizhou, Wenzhou, Ningde, Fuzhou, Quanzhou, Xiamen, Shantou, Shanwei, Shenzhen, Guangzhou, Foshan, Kaiping, Yangjiang, Maoming, Zhanjiang, Haikou
Connecting lines: G1511 (Rizhao-Lankao), G1512 (Ningbo-Jinhua), G1513 (Wenzhou-Lishui), G1514 (Ningde-Shangrao), G1515 (Yancheng-Jingjiang), G1516 (Yancheng-Luoyang), G1517 (Putian-Yanling), G1518 (Yancheng-Bengbu), G1519 (Nantong-Rudong), G1531 (Shanghai-Cixi), G1532 (Quanzhou-Meizhou), G1533 (Quanzhou-Jinmen), G1534 (Xiamen-Jinmen), G1535 (Chaozhou-Nanchang), G1536 (Dongguan-Guangzhou)
Parallel lines: G1521 (Changshu-Jiashan), G1522 (Changshu-Taizhou), G1523 (Ningbo-Dongguan)

▲ G15沈海高速汕头海湾大桥
Shantou Bay Bridge on G15 Shenhai Expressway

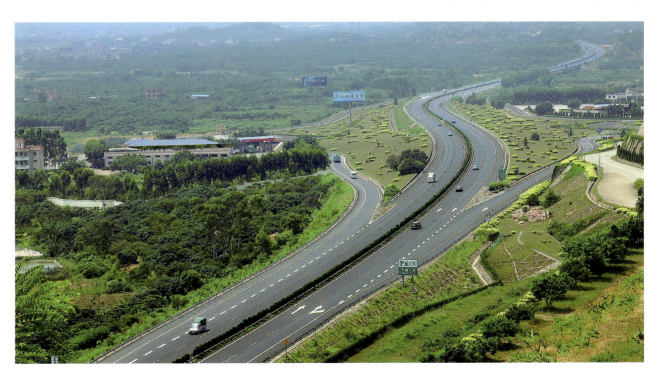

▶ G15沈海高速福建段
Fujian Section of G15 Shenhai Expressway

▲ G1523宁波—东莞高速象山港大桥
Xiangshan Port Bridge on G1523 Ningbo-Dongguan Expressway

G15 沈海高速是国家高速公路网 11 条北南纵线中的第二纵,是连接辽宁、山东、江苏、上海、浙江、福建、广东、海南的重要省际大通道。G15 贯通中国东部沿海地区,是我国最重要的沿海高速公路,沟通了沿海主要港口,促进了港口之间的功能互补与腹地共享,对临海产业带的形成起到重要作用。1990 年建成的沈阳至大连段(沈大高速)是当时中国最长的高速公路,被誉为"神州第一路"。

G15 Shenhai Expressway is the second vertical line of the 11 north-south vertical lines in the national expressway network, and it is an important inter-provincial corridor connecting Liaoning, Shandong, Jiangsu, Shanghai, Zhejiang, Fujian, Guangdong and Hainan. G15 Shenhai Expressway passes through China's eastern coastal area, and it is the most important coastal expressway in China. The Shenyang-Dalian section (Shenda Expressway) completed in 1990 was the longest expressway in China at that time.

NORTH-SOUTH VERTICAL LINE 北 南 纵 线

▲ G15沈海高速杭州湾跨海大桥
Hangzhou Bay Bridge on G15 Shenhai Expressway

▶ G15沈海高速驿坂服务区
Yiban Service Area along G15 Shenhai Expressway

G25 长春—深圳高速公路
Changchun-Shenzhen Expressway

▲ G2518深圳—岑溪高速深中通道
Shenzhong Passage on G2518 Shenzhen–Cenxi Expressway

NORTH-SOUTH VERTICAL LINE　　　　　　　　　　　　　　　　　　　　　　　　　　　　　　　　北　南　纵　线

名　　　称：长春—深圳高速公路（长深高速）
编　　　号：G25
主要控制点：长春、双辽、阜新、朝阳、承德、唐山、天津、黄骅、滨州、青州、连云港、淮安、南京、溧阳、宜兴、湖州、杭州、金华、丽水、南平、三明、梅州、河源、惠州、深圳
联　络　线：G2511（新民—鲁北）、G2512（阜新—锦州）、G2513（淮安—徐州）、G2515（鲁北—霍林郭勒）、G2516（东营—吕梁）、G2517（沙县—厦门）、G2518（深圳—岑溪）、G2519（康平—沈阳）、G2531（杭州—上饶）

Name: Changchun-Shenzhen Expressway (Changshen Expressway)
Number: G25
Main control points: Changchun, Shuangliao, Fuxin, Chaoyang, Chengde, Tangshan, Tianjin, Huanghua, Binzhou, Qingzhou, Lianyungang, Huai'an, Nanjing, Liyang, Yixing, Huzhou, Hangzhou, Jinhua, Lishui, Nanping, Sanming, Meizhou, Heyuan, Huizhou, Shenzhen
Connecting lines: G2511 (Xinmin-Lubei), G2512 (Fuxin-Jinzhou), G2513 (Huai'an-Xuzhou), G2515 (Lubei-Huolin Gol), G2516 (Dongying-Lvliang), G2517 (Shaxian-Xiamen), G2518 (Shenzhen-Cenxi), G2519 (Kangping-Shenyang), G2531 (Hangzhou-Shangrao)

▲ G25长深高速李家巷枢纽
Lijiaxiang Junction on G25 Changshen Expressway

041

▲ G25长深高速南京栖霞山长江大桥
Nanjing Qixiashan Yangtze River Bridge on G25 Changshen Expressway

▲ G25长深高速马站枢纽
Mazhan Junction on G25 Changshen Expressway

NORTH-SOUTH VERTICAL LINE 北 南 纵 线

G25长深高速是国家高速公路网11条北南纵线中的第三纵，连接吉林、内蒙古、辽宁、河北、天津、山东、江苏、安徽、浙江、福建、广东，是贯通东部沿海省份腹地的高速公路通道，也是环渤海、长江三角洲和珠江三角洲三大都市圈的第二条高速公路通道，对于完善国家高速公路网、促进沿线社会经济发展具有重要意义。

G25 Changshen Expressway is the third vertical line of the 11 north-south vertical lines in the national expressway network, connecting Jilin, Inner Mongolia, Liaoning, Hebei, Tianjin, Shandong, Jiangsu, Anhui, Zhejiang, Fujian and Guangdong, and it is an expressway corridor through the hinterland of the eastern coastal provinces. It is also the second expressway corridor in the three metropolitan areas of Bohai Rim, Yangtze River Delta and Pearl River Delta, and is of great significance in improving the national highway network and promoting social and economic development of the areas along the route.

◀ G25长深高速天津海河特大桥
Tianjin Haihe Grand Bridge of G25 ChangShen Expressway

G35 济南—广州高速公路
Jinan-Guangzhou Expressway

▲ G35济广高速天柱山立交桥
Tianzhushan Interchange on G35 Jiguang Expressway

名　　称：	济南—广州高速公路（济广高速）
编　　号：	G35
主要控制点：	济南、菏泽、商丘、阜阳、六安、潜山、望江、景德镇、鹰潭、南城、瑞金、河源、广州
联　络　线：	G3511（菏泽—宝鸡）、G3512（寻乌—赣州）

Name: Jinan-Guangzhou Expressway (Jiguang Expressway)
Number: G35
Main control points: Jinan, Heze, Shangqiu, Fuyang, Lu'an, Qianshan, Wangjiang, Jingdezhen, Yingtan, Nancheng, Ruijin, Heyuan, Guangzhou
Connecting lines: G3511 (Heze-Baoji), G3512 (Xunwu-Ganzhou)

NORTH-SOUTH VERTICAL LINE　　　　　　北　南　纵　线

▼ **G35济广高速零点立交桥**
"Zero Point" Interchange on G35 Jiguang Expressway

▲ G35济广高速安徽段
Anhui Section of G35 Jiguang Expressway

NORTH-SOUTH VERTICAL LINE

北 南 纵 线

G35 济广高速是国家高速公路网 11 条北南纵线中的第四纵，是连接山东、河南、安徽、江西、广东的重要省际大通道。G35 济广高速纵贯华东、华中、华南，直达珠江三角洲，是我国贯穿南北的又一条大通道。

G35 Jiguang Expressway is the fourth vertical line of the 11 north-south vertical lines in the national expressway network, and it is an important inter-provincial corridor connecting Shandong, Henan, Anhui, Jiangxi and Guangdong. G35 Jiguang Expressway runs through the East, Central and South China and directly reaches the Pearl River Delta. It is another major corridor running through the north and south of China.

▲ G3511菏泽—宝鸡高速逢石河大桥
Fengshi River Bridge on G3511 Heze-Baoji Expressway

G45 大庆—广州高速公路
Daqing–Guangzhou Expressway

NORTH-SOUTH VERTICAL LINE　　北 南 纵 线

▲ G45大广高速泰和枢纽立交
Taihe Junction Interchange on G45 Daguang Expressway

名　　　称：	大庆—广州高速公路（大广高速）
编　　　号：	G45
主要控制点：	大庆、松原、双辽、通辽、赤峰、承德、北京、霸州、衡水、濮阳、开封、周口、麻城、黄石、吉安、赣州、龙南、连平、广州
联　络　线：	G4511（龙南—河源）、G4512（双辽—嫩江）、G4513（奈曼旗—营口）、G4515（赤峰—绥中）

Name: Daqing-Guangzhou Expressway (Daguang Expressway)
Number: G45
Main control points: Daqing, Songyuan, Shuangliao, Tongliao, Chifeng, Chengde, Beijing, Bazhou, Hengshui, Puyang, Kaifeng, Zhoukou, Macheng, Huangshi, Ji'an, Ganzhou, Longnan, Lianping, Guangzhou
Connecting lines: G4511 (Longnan-Heyuan), G4512 (Shuangliao-Nenjiang), G4513 (Naiman Banner-Yingkou), G4515 (Chifeng-Suizhong)

◀ G45大广高速黄龙带特大桥
Huanglongdai Grand Bridge on G45 Daguang Expressway

G45大广高速是国家高速公路网11条北南纵线中的第五纵，是连接黑龙江、吉林、内蒙古、河北、北京、河南、湖北、江西、广东的重要省际大通道。G45大广高速是连接东北、华北、华中与华南的交通大动脉，对于加强东北、华北地区与华南地区之间的经济联系、促进沿线经济的发展具有重大意义。G45大广高速是东北与华北联系的第三条通道，对改善路网布局起着重要作用。

G45 Daguang Expressway is the fifth vertical line of the 11 north-south vertical lines in the national expressway network, and it is an important inter-provincial corridor connecting Heilongjiang, Jilin, Inner Mongolia, Hebei, Beijing, Henan, Hubei, Jiangxi and Guangdong. G45 Daguang Expressway is the transportation artery connecting Northeast, North, Central and South China. It has great significance in strengthening economic ties between Northeast, North and South China, and promoting the economic development along the route. G45 Daguang Expressway is the third channel connecting Northeast and North China, which plays an important role in improving the road network layout.

▲ G45大广高速江西段
Jiangxi Section of G45 Daguang Expressway

▲ G45大广高速鄂东长江大桥
E'dong Yangtze River Bridge on G45 Daguang Expressway

NORTH-SOUTH VERTICAL LINE 北 南 纵 线

▲ G45大广高速吕田服务区
Lvtian Service Area along G45 Daguang Expressway

二连浩特—广州高速公路
Erenhot–Guangzhou Expressway

▲ **G55二广高速荆门互通**
Jingmen Interchange on G55 Erguang Expressway

G55 二广高速是国家高速公路网 11 条北南纵线中的第六纵，是连接内蒙古、山西、河南、湖北、湖南、广东的重要省际大通道，是纵贯中国中部地区的南北大动脉，也是 G4 京港澳高速的重要辅助通道，对于缓解交通压力，改善路网布局具有重要的意义。

G55 Erguang Expressway is the sixth vertical line of the 11 north-south vertical lines in the national expressway network, and it is an important inter-provincial corridor connecting Inner Mongolia, Shanxi, Henan, Hubei, Hunan and Guangdong. It is a major north-south artery running through the central region of China, and is an important auxiliary corridor of G4 Jinggang'ao Expressway. It has an important significance in easing the traffic pressure and improving the layout of the road network.

▲ G55二广高速广东段
Guangdong Section of G55 Erguang Expressway

▲ G55二广高速九嶷山隧道
Jiuyishan Tunnel on G55 Erguang Expressway

G55二广高速荆州长江大桥
Jingzhou Yangtze River Bridge on G55 Erguang Expressway

NORTH-SOUTH VERTICAL LINE　　●—○　北 南 纵 线

▲ G55二广高速龙城服务区
Longcheng Service Area along G55 Erguang Expressway

名　　称：二连浩特—广州高速公路（二广高速）
编　　号：G55
主要控制点：二连浩特、集宁、大同、太原、长治、晋城、洛阳、南召、南阳、襄阳、荆州、常德、娄底、邵阳、永州、连州、广州
联　络　线：G5511（集宁—阿荣旗）、G5512（晋城—新乡）、G5513（长沙—张家界）、G5515（张家界—南充）、G5516（苏尼特右旗—张家口）、G5517（常德—长沙）、G5518（晋城—潼关）

Name: Erenhot-Guangzhou Expressway (Erguang Expressway)
Number: G55
Main control points: Erenhot, Jining, Datong, Taiyuan, Changzhi, Jincheng, Luoyang, Nanzhao, Nanyang, Xiangyang, Jingzhou, Changde, Loudi, Shaoyang, Yongzhou, Lianzhou, Guangzhou
Connecting lines: G5511 (Jining-Arong Banner), G5512 (Jincheng-Xinxiang), G5513 (Changsha -Zhangjiajie), G5515 (Zhangjiajie-Nanchong), G5516 (Sunite Right Banner-Zhangjiakou), G5517 (Changde-Changsha), G5518 (Jincheng-Tongguan)

G59 呼和浩特—北海高速公路
Hohhot–Beihai Expressway

▲ G59呼北高速平南北枢纽
Pingnanbei Junction on G59 Hubei Expressway

NORTH-SOUTH VERTICAL LINE 北 南 纵 线

▲ G59呼北高速湖北段
Hubei section of G59 Hubei Expressway

▲ G59呼北高速广西段
Guangxi Section of G59 Hubei Expressway

名　　　称：	呼和浩特—北海高速公路（呼北高速）
编　　　号：	G59
主要控制点：	呼和浩特、和林格尔、右玉、朔州、岢岚、吕梁、吉县、运城、灵宝、卢氏、十堰、房县、保康、宜都、慈利、张家界、新化、武冈、新宁、资源、荔浦、平南、玉林、北海（铁山港）
联　络　线：	G5911（朔州—太原）、G5912（房县—五峰）

▲ G59呼北高速河南段
Henan Section of G59 Hubei Expressway

▲ G59呼北高速运宝黄河大桥
Yunbao Yellow River Bridge on G59 Hubei Expressway

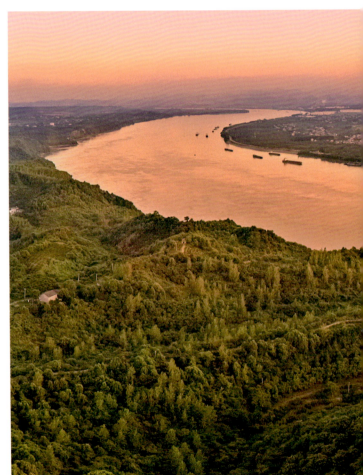

NORTH-SOUTH VERTICAL LINE

Name: Hohhot-Beihai Expressway (Hubei Expressway)
Number: G59
Main control points: Hohhot, Helingeer, Youyu, Shuozhou, Kelan, Lvliang, Jixian, Yuncheng, Lingbao, Lushi, Shiyan, Fangxian, Baokang, Yidu, Cili, Zhangjiajie, Xinhua, Wugang, Xinning, Ziyuan, Lipu, Pingnan, Yulin, Beihai (Tieshangang)
Connecting lines: G5911 (Shuozhou-Taiyuan), G5912 (Fangxian-Wufeng)

G59 呼北高速是国家高速公路网 11 条北南纵线中的第七纵，是连接内蒙古、山西、河南、湖北、湖南、广西的重要省际大通道，是"71118+6"规划与"7918"规划相比新增的两条纵线之一，对于加强中西部地区交流合作、改善中西部山区交通条件具有重要意义。

G59 Hubei Expressway is the seventh vertical line of the 11 north-south vertical lines in the national expressway network, and it is an important inter-provincial corridor connecting Inner Mongolia, Shanxi, Henan, Hubei, Hunan and Guangxi. It is of great significance for strengthening the communication and cooperation between the central and western regions, and improving the transportation conditions of the mountainous areas in the central and western regions.

▲ G59呼北高速宜都长江大桥
Yidu Yangtze River Bridge on G59 Hubei Expressway

G65 包头—茂名高速公路
Baotou–Maoming Expressway

G65包茂高速与S99龙吉高速互通
Interchange between G65 Baomao Expressway and S99 Longji Expressway

▲ G65包茂高速陕西段
Shaanxi Section of G65 Baomao Expressway

名　　　称：包头—茂名高速公路（包茂高速）
编　　　号：G65
主要控制点：包头、鄂尔多斯、榆林、延安、铜川、西安、安康、达州、重庆、黔江、吉首、怀化、桂林、梧州、茂名
联　络　线：G6511（安塞—清涧）、G6512（秀山—从江）、G6517（梧州—柳州）
并　行　线：G6521（榆林—蓝田）、G6522（延安—西安）

Name: Baotou-Maoming Expressway (Baomao Expressway)
Number: G65
Main control points: Baotou, Ordos, Yulin, Yan'an, Tongchuan, Xi'an, Ankang, Dazhou, Chongqing, Qianjiang, Jishou, Huaihua, Guilin, Wuzhou, Maoming
Connecting lines: G6511 (Ansai-Qingjian), G6512 (Xiushan-Congjiang), G6517 (Wuzhou-Liuzhou)
Parallel lines: G6521 (Yulin-Lantian), G6522 (Yan'an-Xi'an)

◀ G65包茂高速白马隧道群
Baima Tunnel Group on G65 Baomao Expressway

NORTH-SOUTH VERTICAL LINE 北 南 纵 线

G65 包茂高速是国家高速公路网 11 条北南纵线中的第八纵，是连接内蒙古、陕西、四川、重庆、湖南、广西、广东的重要省际大通道。连接西北、西南与华南地区，通江达海，是重要的西部开发公路通道，在西部大开发战略中起到了不可忽视的作用。

G65 Baomao Expressway is the eighth vertical line of the 11 north-south vertical lines in the national expressway network, and it is an important inter-provincial corridor connecting Inner Mongolia, Shaanxi, Sichuan, Chongqing, Hunan, Guangxi and Guangdong. It connects Northwest, Southwest and South China, and plays an indispensable role in China's western development strategy.

▲ G65包茂高速矮寨大桥
Aizhai Bridge on G65 Baomao Expressway

▲ G65包茂高速叠石花谷景区服务区
Dieshihua Valley Scenic Service Area along G65 Baomao Expressway

G69 银川—百色高速公路
Yinchuan–Baise Expressway

▲ G6911安康—来凤高速白杨坪枢纽互通
Baiyangping Hub Interchange on G6911 Ankang–Laifeng Expressway

NORTH-SOUTH VERTICAL LINE 北 南 纵 线

▲ G69银百高速与S60合那高速互通
Interchange between G69 Yinbai Expressway and S60 Hena Expressway

名　　　称：银川—百色高速公路（银百高速）
编　　　号：G69
主要控制点：银川、惠安堡、庆城、旬邑、西安、安康、岚皋、城口、万州、忠县、涪陵、南川、道真、瓮安、贵阳、罗甸、乐业、百色（龙邦口岸）
联　络　线：G6911（安康—来凤）

Name: Yinchuan-Baise Expressway (Yinbai Expressway)
Number: G69
Main control points: Yinchuan, Hui'anbu, Qingcheng, Xunyi, Xi'an, Ankang, Langao, Chengkou, Wanzhou, Zhongxian, Fuling, Nanchuan, Daozhen, Weng'an, Guiyang, Luodian, Leye, Baise (Longbang Checkpoint)
Connecting line: G6911 (Ankang-Laifeng)

G69 银百高速是国家高速公路网 11 条北南纵线中的第九纵，是连接宁夏、甘肃、陕西、重庆、贵州、广西的重要省际大通道，是沟通西北、西南地区，连接龙邦口岸，通往东南亚的重要公路通道。

G69 Yinbai Expressway is the ninth vertical line of the 11 north-south vertical lines in the national expressway network, and it is an important inter-provincial corridor connecting Ningxia, Gansu, Shaanxi, Chongqing, Guizhou and Guangxi. It communicates with Northwest and Southwest China, connects Longbang checkpoint, and is an important highway channel to Southeast Asia.

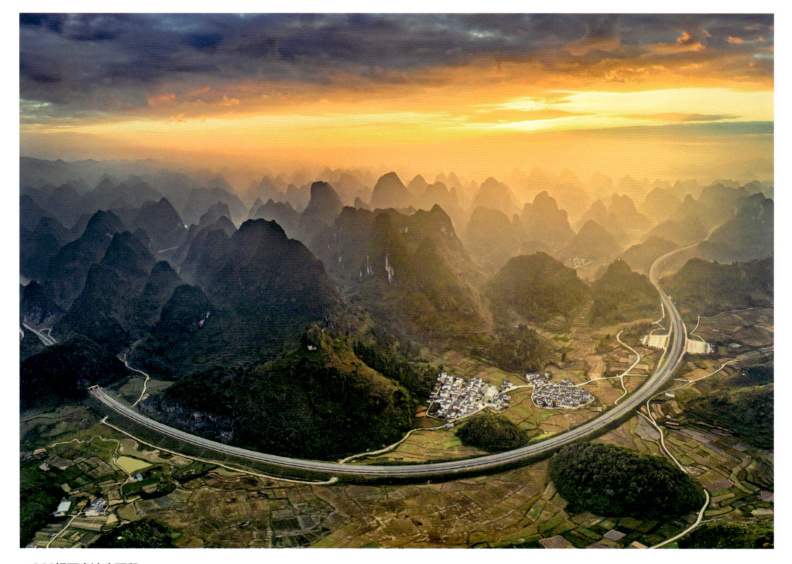

▲ G69银百高速广西段
Guangxi Section of G69 Yinbai Expressway

▲ G69银百高速贵州段
Guizhou Section of G69 Yinbai Expressway

▲ G69银百高速清水河大桥
Qingshui River Bridge on G69 Yinbai Expressway

▲ G69银百高速湄潭东服务区
Meitan East Service Area along G69 Yinbai Expressway

G75 兰州—海口高速公路
Lanzhou-Haikou Expressway

名　　称：兰州—海口高速公路（兰海高速）
编　　号：G75
主要控制点：兰州、广元、南充、重庆、遵义、贵阳、麻江、都匀、河池、南宁、钦州、北海、湛江、海口
联 络 线：G7511（钦州—东兴）、G7512（贵阳—成都）
并 行 线：G7521（重庆—贵阳）、G7522（贵阳—北海）

Name: Lanzhou-Haikou Expressway (Lanhai Expressway)
Number: G75
Main control points: Lanzhou, Guangyuan, Nanchong, Chongqing, Zunyi, Guiyang, Majiang, Duyun, Hechi, Nanning, Qinzhou, Beihai, Zhanjiang, Haikou
Connecting lines: G7511 (Qinzhou – Dongxing), G7512 (Guiyang – Chengdu)
Parallel lines: G7521 (Chongqing – Guiyang), G7522 (Guiyang – Beihai)

▲ G7521重庆—贵阳高速蒲场特大桥
Puchang Grand Bridge on G7521 Chongqing – Guiyang Expressway

▲ G7521重庆—贵阳高速马鬃互通
Mazong Interchange on G7521 Chongqing – Guiyang Expressway

▲ G75兰海高速广西段
Guangxi Section of G75 Lanhai Expressway

　　G75 兰海高速是国家高速公路网 11 条北南纵线中的第十纵，是连接甘肃、四川、重庆、贵州、广西、广东、海南的重要省际大通道。沟通西北、西南与华南地区，是西北与西南地区出海大通道的主通道。对于改善西部地区交通条件、完善路网结构、均衡国土开发均具有十分重要的作用。

G75 Lanhai Expressway is the tenth vertical line of the 11 north-south vertical lines in the national expressway network, and it is an important inter-provincial corridor connecting Gansu, Sichuan, Chongqing, Guizhou, Guangxi, Guangdong and Hainan. It communicates with the Northwest, Southwest and South China, and is the main channel of the sea access in the Northwest and Southwest China. It plays a very important role for the improvement of transportation conditions in the western region and the improvement of the road network structure, as well as for balancing the development of land.

▲ G7521重庆—贵阳高速楠木渡乌江大桥
Nanmudu Wujiang Bridge on G7521 Chongqing – Guiyang Expressway

▲ G7521重庆—贵阳高速大娄山隧道
Daloushan Tunnel on G7521 Chongqing – Guiyang Expressway

▲ G75兰海高速岷县服务区
Minxian Service Area along G75 Lanhai Expressway

G85 银川—昆明高速公路
Yinchuan–Kunming Expressway

▼ G85银昆高速与G8513平绵高速互通
Interchange between G85 Yinkun Expressway and G8513 Pingmian Expressway

G85银昆高速是国家高速公路网11条南北纵线中的第十一纵，是连接宁夏、甘肃、陕西、四川、重庆、云南的重要省际大通道。原"7918"规划中的G85（渝昆高速）起于重庆，根据"71118"规划，该路段向北延伸至银川，形成了现在的G85（银昆高速）。G85（银昆高速）对缓解西部地区南北向的交通运输压力具有十分积极的作用，促进了西部地区经济发展，加强了中西部地区的联系与交流，是这一地区的重要通道。

G85 Yinkun Expressway is the eleventh vertical line of the 11 north-south vertical lines in the national expressway network, and it is an important inter-provincial corridor connecting Ningxia, Gansu, Shaanxi, Sichuan, Chongqing and Yunnan. G85 Yinkun Expressway has a very positive role in easing the pressure of north-south transportation in the western region, promoting the economic development of the western region, and strengthening the links and exchanges between the central and western regions. It is an important corridor in this region.

▲ G8513平凉—绵阳高速甘肃段
Gansu Section of G8513 Pingliang-Mianyang Expressway

▶ G8516巴中—成都高速四川段
Sichuan Section of G8516 Bazhong-Chengdu Expressway

NORTH-SOUTH VERTICAL LINE 北 南 纵 线

名　　称：银川—昆明高速公路（银昆高速）
编　　号：G85
主要控制点：银川、惠安堡、彭阳、平凉、华亭、宝鸡、留坝、汉中、巴中、广安、重庆、内江、宜宾、昭通、昆明
联 络 线：G8511（昆明—磨憨）、G8512（景洪—打洛）、G8513（平凉—绵阳）、G8515（广安—泸州）、
　　　　　G8516（巴中—成都）、G8517（屏山—兴义）

Name: Yinchuan-Kunming Expressway (Yinkun Expressway)
Number: G85
Main control points: Yinchuan, Hui'anbu, Pengyang, Pingliang, Huating, Baoji, Liuba, Hanzhong, Bazhong, Guang'an, Chongqing, Neijiang, Yibin, Zhaotong, Kunming
Connecting lines: G8511 (Kunming – Mohan), G8512 (Jinghong – Daluo), G8513 (Pingliang – Mianyang), G8515 (Guang'an – Luzhou), G8516 (Bazhong – Chengdu), G8517 (Pingshan – Xingyi)

▼ G85银昆高速秦岭天台山隧道
Qinling Tiantaishan Tunnel on G85 Yinkun Expressway

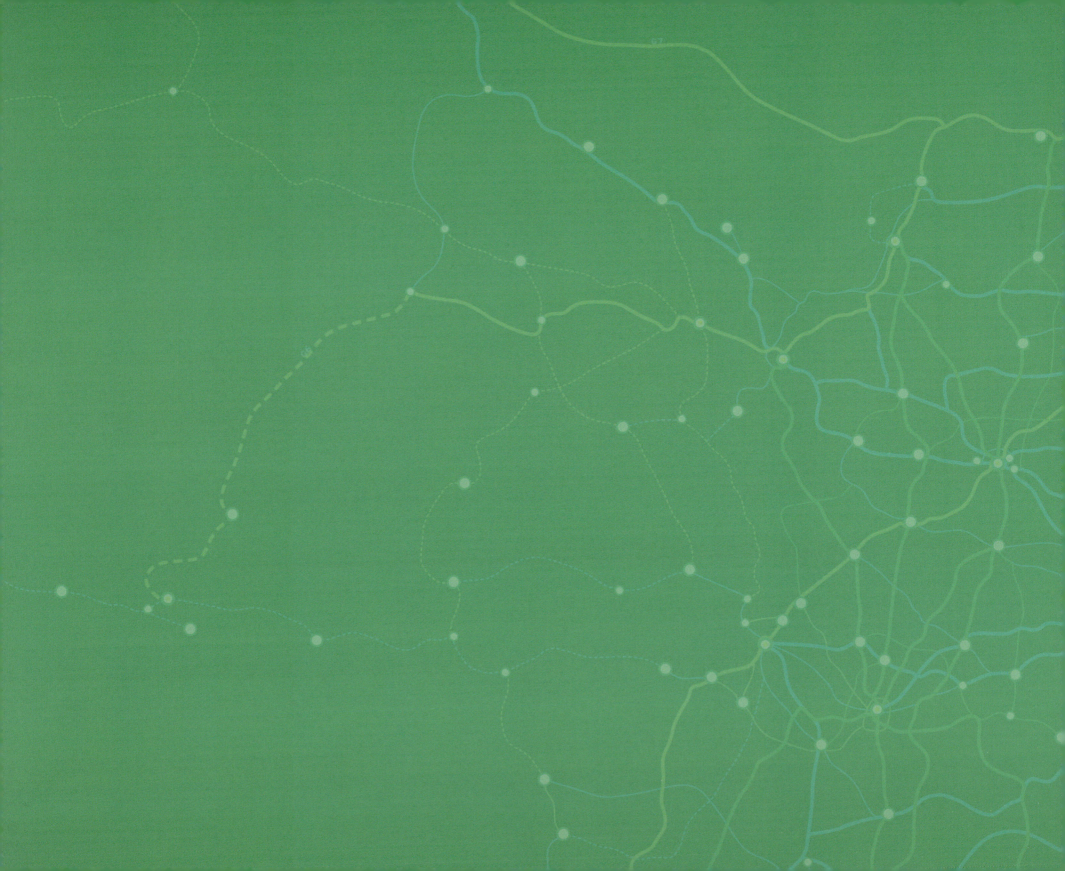

东西横线

EAST-WEST HORIZONTAL LINE

G10	G12	G16	G18
G20	G22	G30	G36
G40	G42	G50	G56
G60	G70	G72	G76
		G78	G80

中国高速公路

EXPRESSWAYS IN CHINA

G10 绥芬河—满洲里高速公路
Suifenhe-Manzhouli Expressway

▲ G10绥满高速黑龙江段
　Heilongjiang Section of G10 Suiman Expressway

EAST-WEST HORIZONTAL LINE 东 西 横 线

G10绥满高速是国家高速公路网18条东西横线中的第一横，经过绥芬河、东宁、满洲里三个一类口岸。G10绥满高速与干线连同其联络线和地方高速公路形成了黑龙江省的高速公路网络，是连接边境口岸和重要城市的经济战略通道，进一步扩大口岸的辐射范围，对繁荣口岸经济和国际贸易起到重要作用。

G10 Suiman Expressway is the first horizontal line of the 18 east-west horizontal lines in the national expressway network, passing through three first-class checkpoints, which are Suifenhe, Dongning and Manzhouli. G10 Suiman Expressway and the trunk line, together with its liaison line and local highway, form the expressway network of Heilongjiang province. It is an economic and strategic channel connecting the border checkpoints and important cities.

▲ G10绥满高速四方台大桥
Sifangtai Bridge on G10 Suiman Expressway

▲ G10绥满高速卧里屯收费站
Wolitun Toll Station on G10 Suiman Expressway

名　　称：绥芬河—满洲里高速公路（绥满高速）	**Name:** Suifenhe-Manzhouli Expressway (Suiman Expressway)
编　　号：G10	**Number:** G10
主要控制点：绥芬河（口岸）、牡丹江、哈尔滨、大庆、齐齐哈尔、阿荣旗、满洲里（口岸）	**Main control points:** Suifenhe (checkpoint), Mudanjiang, Harbin, Daqing, Qiqihar, Arong Banner, Manzhouli (checkpoint)
联 络 线：G1011（哈尔滨—同江）、G1012（建三江—黑瞎子岛）、G1013（海拉尔—张家口）、G1015（铁力—科尔沁右翼中旗）、G1016（双鸭山—宝清）、G1017（海拉尔—加格达奇）	**Connecting lines:** G1011 (Harbin-Tongjiang), G1012 (Jiansanjiang-Heixiazi Island), G1013 (Hailar-Zhangjiakou), G1015 (Tieli-Horqin Right Wing Middle Banner), G1016 (Shuangyashan-Baoqing), G1017 (Hailar-Jiagedaqi)

EAST-WEST HORIZONTAL LINE 东 西 横 线

▲ G10绥满高速安达服务区
Anda Service Area along G10 Suiman Expressway

G12 珲春—乌兰浩特高速公路
Hunchun-Ulanhot Expressway

名　　称：珲春—乌兰浩特高速公路（珲乌高速）
编　　号：G12
主要控制点：珲春（防川）、敦化、吉林、长春、松原、白城、乌兰浩特
联　络　线：G1211（吉林—黑河）、G1212（沈阳—吉林）、G1213（北安—漠河）、G1215（松江—长白山）、G1216（乌兰浩特—阿力得尔）
并　行　线：G1221（延吉—长春）

Name: Hunchun-Ulanhot Expressway (Hunwu Expressway)
Number: G12
Main control points: Hunchun (Fangchuan), Dunhua, Jilin, Changchun, Songyuan, Baicheng, Ulanhot
Connecting lines: G1211 (Jilin-Heihe), G1212 (Shenyang-Jilin), G1213 (Bei'an-Mohe), G1215 (Songjiang-Changbaishan), G1216 (Ulanhot-Arider)
Parallel line: G1221 (Yanji-Changchun)

▲ G12珲乌高速江密峰镇互通
Jiangmifeng Town Interchange on G12 Hunwu Expressway

▲ G1211吉林—黑河高速兰旗大桥
Lanqi Bridge on G1211 Jilin-Heihe Expressway

G12 珲乌高速是国家高速公路网 18 条东西横线中的第二横，位于东北地区中部，经过重要口岸珲春，是连接边境口岸和重要城市的经济通道，是黑龙江西南、内蒙古东北和吉林西部等经济区出海的便捷通道，为区域资源开发、旅游产业发展提供方便快捷的交通条件。

G12 Hunwu Expressway is the second horizontal line of the 18 east-west horizontal lines in the national expressway network. It is an economic channel connecting the border checkpoints and important cities, and is a convenient channel for the economic zones of southwestern Heilongjiang, northeastern Inner Mongolia, and western Jilin to go out to the sea. It provides convenient and fast transportation conditions for the regional development of resources and the development of the tourism industry.

▲ G12珲乌高速长安隧道
Chang'an Tunnel on G12 Hunwu Expressway

中国高速公路 — EXPRESSWAYS IN CHINA

丹东—锡林浩特高速公路
Dandong-Xilinhot Expressway

名　　　称：丹东—锡林浩特高速公路（丹锡高速）
编　　　号：G16
主要控制点：丹东、海城、盘锦、锦州、朝阳、赤峰、克什克腾旗、锡林浩特
联　络　线：G1611（克什克腾—承德）、G1612（锡林浩特—二连浩特）

Name: Dandong-Xilinhot Expressway (Danxi Expressway)
Number: G16
Main control points: Dandong, Haicheng, Panjin, Jinzhou, Chaoyang, Chifeng, Keshiketeng Banner, Xilinhot
Connecting lines: G1611（Keshiketeng-Chengde), G1612（Xilinhot-Erlianhot)

▼ G16丹锡高速与G207锡林浩特绕城公路互通
Interchange between G16 Danxi Expressway and G207 Xilinhot Urban Ring Road

EAST-WEST HORIZONTAL LINE 东 西 横 线

▲ G16丹锡高速集锡线交汇处
Jixi Interchange on G16 Danxi Expressway

　　G16 丹锡高速是国家高速公路网 18 条东西横线中的第三横，是连接边境口岸、重要工业城市和内蒙古草原的重要经济通道，也是内蒙古东部主要出海通道，对促进沿线地区资源开发和经济社会协调发展具有重要的意义。

G16 Danxi Expressway is the third horizontal line of the 18 east-west horizontal lines in the national expressway network. It is an important economic channel connecting the border checkpoints, important industrial cities and Inner Mongolia grassland, and is the main seaward channel of the eastern Inner Mongolia. It is of great significance in promoting the development of resources and coordinated economic and social development of the areas along the route.

◀ G16丹锡高速克什克腾旗境内
G16 Danxi Expressway in Keshketeng Banner

G18 荣成—乌海高速公路
Rongcheng-Wuhai Expressway

名　　称：荣成—乌海高速公路（荣乌高速）
编　　号：G18
主要控制点：荣成、文登、威海、烟台、东营、黄骅、天津、霸州、涞源、朔州、鄂尔多斯、乌海
联 络 线：G1811（黄骅—石家庄）、G1812（沧州—榆林）、G1813（威海—青岛）、G1815（潍坊—日照）、G1816（乌海—玛沁）、G1817（乌海—银川）、G1818（滨州—德州）

Name: Rongcheng-Wuhai Expressway (Rongwu Expressway)
Number: G18
Main control points: Rongcheng, Wendeng, Weihai, Yantai, Dongying, Huanghua, Tianjin, Bazhou, Laiyuan, Shuozhou, Ordos, Wuhai
Connecting lines: G1811（Huanghua - Shijiazhuang）, G1812（Cangzhou - Yulin）, G1813（Weihai - Qingdao）, G1815（Weifang - Rizhao）, G1816（Wuhai - Maqin）, G1817（Wuhai - Yinchuan）, G1818（Binzhou - Dezhou）

▲ G1816乌海—玛沁高速宁夏段
Ningxia Section of G1816 Wuhai-Maqin Expressway

EAST-WEST HORIZONTAL LINE 东 西 横 线

▲ G18荣乌高速大运枢纽
Dayun Junction on G18 Rongwu Expressway

▲ G18荣乌高速与G3京台高速互通
Interchange between G18 Rongwu Expressway and G3 Jingtai Expressway

EAST-WEST HORIZONTAL LINE 东西横线

G18 荣乌高速是国家高速公路网 18 条东西横线中的第四横，是连接华东北部、华北中西部的东西横向干线，是连接环渤海港口工业城市和内蒙古西部的重要通道，也是内蒙古中西部的重要出海通道。

G18 Rongwu Expressway is the fourth horizontal line of the 18 east-west horizontal lines in the national expressway network, and it is the east-west horizontal trunk line connecting the northern part of East China and the central and western part of North China. It is an important passage connecting the port industrial cities around Bohai Rim and western Inner Mongolia, and is also an important seaward corridor in central and western Inner Mongolia.

▲ G18荣乌高速天津站
Tianjin Station of G18 Rongwu Expressway

中国高速公路 — EXPRESSWAYS IN CHINA

青岛—银川高速公路
Qingdao-Yinchuan Expressway

名　　称：青岛—银川高速公路（青银高速）
编　　号：G20
主要控制点：青岛、潍坊、淄博、济南、石家庄、太原、离石、靖边、定边、银川
联 络 线：G2011（青岛—新河）、G2012（定边—武威）

Name: Qingdao-Yinchuan Expressway (Qingyin Expressway)
Number: G20
Main control points: Qingdao, Weifang, Zibo, Jinan, Shijiazhuang, Taiyuan, Lishi, Jingbian, Dingbian, Yinchuan
Connecting lines: G2011 (Qingdao – Xinhe), G2012 (Dingbian – Wuwei)

▼ G20青银高速与S9902新元高速互通
Interchange between G20 Qingyin Expressway and S9902 Xinyuan Expressway

G20 青银高速是国家高速公路网 18 条东西横线中的第五横，是连接东部沿海城市和中西部地区的重要通道，连接着西北地区和华北地区的诸多大中城市，是西北地区重要的出海通道，对于加强西北内陆和东部沿海之间相互连通，促进沿线地区的经济社会发展发挥着巨大作用。

G20 Qingyin Expressway is the fifth horizontal line of the 18 east-west horizontal lines in the national expressway network, and it is an important corridor connecting the eastern coastal cities and the central and western regions, as well as connecting many large and medium-sized cities in Northwest and North China. It is an important seaward corridor in Northwest China, and it plays a great role in strengthening the intercommunication between northwest inland and the eastern seaboard, and in promoting the economic and social development of the areas along the route.

▼ G20青银高速银川黄河大桥
Yinchuan Yellow River Bridge on G20 Qingyin Expressway

G22 青岛—兰州高速公路
Qingdao–Lanzhou Expressway

名　　称：青岛—兰州高速公路（青兰高速）
编　　号：G22
主要控制点：青岛、莱芜、泰安、聊城、邯郸、长治、临汾、富县、庆阳、平凉、定西、兰州
联　络　线：G2211（长治—延安）

Name: Qingdao-Lanzhou Expressway (Qinglan Expressway)
Number: G22
Main control points: Qingdao, Laiwu, Tai'an, Liaocheng, Handan, Changzhi, Linfen, Fuxian, Qingyang, Pingliang, Dingxi, Lanzhou
Connecting line: G2211 (Changzhi – Yan'an)

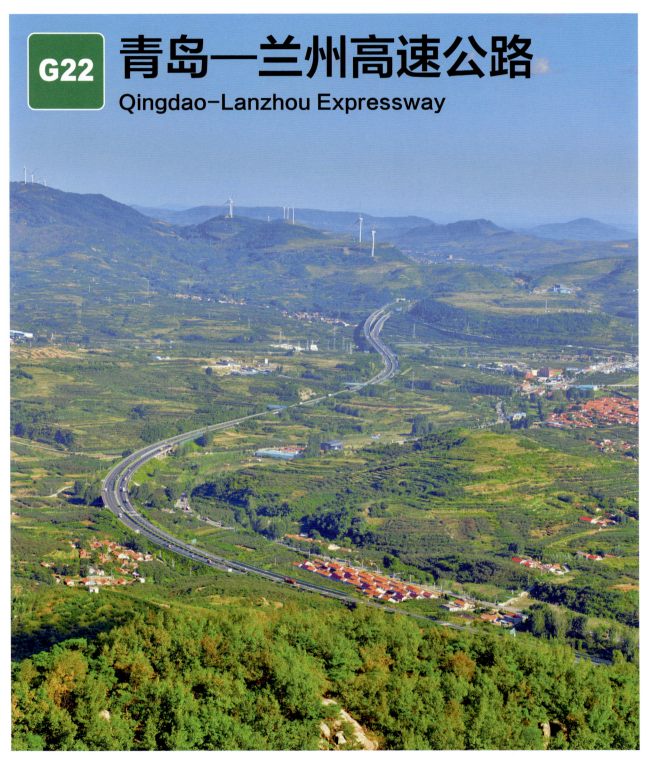

　　G22 青兰高速是国家高速公路网 18 条东西横线中的第六横，是一条连接华东北部、华北和西北的东西横向干线，也是西北地区的第二条出海通道。

G22 Qinglan Expressway is the sixth horizontal line of the 18 east-west horizontal lines in the national expressway network. It is an east-west horizontal trunk line connecting the north part of East China, as well as North and Northwest China, and is also the second sea access in Northwest China.

◀ **G22青兰高速山东段**
Shandong Section of G22 Qinglan Expressway

◀ G22青兰高速吉县黄河特大桥
Jixian Yellow River Grand Bridge on G22 Qinglan Expressway

▼ G22青兰高速兰州东收费站
Lanzhou East Toll Station on G22 Qinglan Expressway

G30 连云港—霍尔果斯高速公路
Lianyungang-Khorgos Expressway

▲ G30连霍高速与G59呼北高速互通
Interchange between G30 Lianhuo Expressway and G59 Hubei Expressway

EAST-WEST HORIZONTAL LINE 东 西 横 线

名　　称：连云港—霍尔果斯高速公路（连霍高速）
编　　号：G30
主要控制点：连云港、徐州、商丘、开封、郑州、洛阳、西安、宝鸡、天水、兰州、武威、嘉峪关、哈密、吐鲁番、乌鲁木齐、奎屯、霍尔果斯（口岸）
联 络 线：G3011（柳园—格尔木）、G3012（吐鲁番—和田）、G3013（阿图什—伊尔克什坦）、G3014（奎屯—阿勒泰）、G3015（奎屯—塔城）、G3016（清水河—伊宁）、G3017（武威—金昌）、G3018（精河—阿拉山口）、G3019（博乐—阿拉山口）、G3031（商丘—固始）、G3032（永登—海晏）、G3033（奎屯—库车）、G3035（伊宁—新源）、G3036（阿克苏—阿拉尔）
并 行 线：G3021（临潼—兴平）

Name: Lianyungang-Khorgos Expressway (Lianhuo Expressway)
Number: G30
Main control points: Lianyungang, Xuzhou, Shangqiu, Kaifeng, Zhengzhou, Luoyang, Xi'an, Baoji, Tianshui, Lanzhou, Wuwei, Jiayuguan, Hami, Turpan, Urumqi, Kuitun, Khorgos (checkpoint)
Connecting lines: G3011 (Liuyuan-Golmud), G3012 (Turpan-Khotan), G3013 (Atush-Irkeshtan) ,G3014 (Kuitun-Altai), G3015 (Kuitun-Tacheng), G3016 (Qingshuihe-Yining), G3017 (Wuwei-Jinchang), G3018 (Jinghe-Alashankou), G3019 (Bole-Alashankou),G3031 (Shangqiu-Gushi), G3032 (Yongdeng-Haiyan), G3033 (Kuitun- Kuche), G3035 (Yining-Xinyuan), G3036 (Aksu- Alar)
Parallel line: G3021 (Lintong- Xingping)

▲ G30连霍高速果子沟大桥
Guozigou Bridge on G30 Lianhuo Expressway

G30 连霍高速是国家高速公路网 18 条东西横线中的第七横，是连接江苏、安徽、河南、陕西、甘肃、新疆的重要省际通道，横贯我国中部地区，是我国最长的一条高速公路。G30 连霍高速东起江苏连云港港区，西至新疆维吾尔自治区霍尔果斯口岸，打通了西北、中原及东部沿海的高速公路通道，是亚欧大陆桥的组成部分。随着我国"一带一路"倡议的提出，G30 连霍高速的作用更加凸显。

G30 Lianhuo Expressway is the seventh horizontal line of the 18 east-west horizontal lines in the national expressway network, and it is an important inter-provincial corridor connecting Jiangsu, Anhui, Henan, Shaanxi, Gansu and Xinjiang. Spreading across the central region of China, it is the longest expressway in China. G30 Lianhuo Expressway opens up the highway corridor between the northwest, central plain and east coast regions in China, and it is a component of the Asia-Europe Continental Bridge. With the proposal of China's Belt and Road Initiative, the role of the G30 Lianhuo Expressway has become even more prominent.

▲ G30连霍高速小草湖互通
Xiaocaohu Interchange on G30 Lianhuo Expressway

G36 南京—洛阳高速公路
Nanjing-Luoyang Expressway

▲ G36宁洛高速雍庄枢纽
Yongzhuang Junction on G36 Ningluo Expressway

名　　　称：南京—洛阳高速公路（宁洛高速）
编　　　号：G36
主要控制点：南京、蚌埠、阜阳、周口、漯河、平顶山、洛阳
联　络　线：G3611（南京—信阳）、G3612（平顶山—宜昌）、G3613（洛阳—内乡）、G3615（洛阳—卢氏）

Name: Nanjing-Luoyang Expressway (Ningluo Expressway)
Number: G36
Main control points: Nanjing, Bengbu, Fuyang, Zhoukou, Luohe, Pingdingshan, Luoyang
Connecting lines: G3611 (Nanjing-Xinyang), G3612 (Pingdingshan-Yichang), G3613 (Luoyang-Neixiang), G3615 (Luoyang-Lushi)

　　G36 宁洛高速是国家高速公路网 18 条东西横线中的第八横，是连接江苏、安徽、河南的重要省际通道，是中原地区连接长三角区域的高速公路运输线，G36 宁洛高速对国土均衡开发、改善路网布局和加快经济社会发展具有重要意义。

G36 Ningluo Expressway is the eighth horizontal line of the 18 east-west horizontal lines in the national expressway network. It is an important inter-provincial corridor connecting Jiangsu, Anhui and Henan, and is an expressway transportation line connecting the Central Plains to the Yangtze River Delta. G36 Ningluo Expressway is of great significance for balancing the development of land, the improvement of road network layout and the acceleration of economic and social development.

▲ G36宁洛高速南京八卦洲长江大桥
Nanjing Baguazhou Yangtze River Bridge on G36 Ningluo Expressway

▶ G36宁洛高速河南段
Henan Section of G36 Ningluo Expressway

G40 上海—西安高速公路
Shanghai-Xi'an Expressway

▲ G4012溧阳—宁德高速杭州段
Hangzhou section of G4012 Liyang-Ningde Expressway

EAST-WEST HORIZONTAL LINE 东西横线

▲ G40沪陕高速上海长江大桥
Shanghai Yangtze River Bridge on G40 Hushan Expressway

G40沪陕高速是国家高速公路网18条东西横线中的第九横，是连接上海、江苏、安徽、河南、陕西的重要省际通道，连接华东、华中与西北地区，显著改善中国西部地区与中东部地区之间的交通条件和经济联系，是长江三角洲都市圈向华中、西北地区辐射的重要高速通道。

G40 Hushan Expressway is the ninth horizontal line of the 18 east-west horizontal lines in the national expressway network. It is an important inter-provincial corridor connecting Shanghai, Jiangsu, Anhui, Henan and Shaanxi, as well as connecting East, Central and Northwest China, significantly improving the transportation conditions and economic ties between the western region and the middle and east regions of China. It is an important high-speed corridor for the Yangtze River Delta metropolitan area to radiate to Central and Northwest China.

▲ G4012溧阳—宁德高速金竹牌大桥
Jinzhupai Bridge on G4012 Liyang-Ningde Expressway

EAST-WEST HORIZONTAL LINE 东 西 横 线

▲ G40沪陕高速沪崇苏互通
Huchongsu Interchange on G40 Hushan Expressway

名　　　称：	上海—西安高速公路（沪陕高速）
编　　　号：	G40
主要控制点：	上海（浦东新区）、崇明、南通、扬州、南京、合肥、六安、信阳、南阳、商州、西安
联 络 线：	G4011（扬州—溧阳）、G4012（溧阳—宁德）、G4013（扬州—乐清）、G4015（丹凤—宁陕）

Name: Shanghai to-Xi'an Expressway (Hushan Expressway)
Number: G40
Main control points: Shanghai (Pudong New Area), Chongming, Nantong, Yangzhou, Nanjing, Hefei, Lu'an, Xinyang, Nanyang, Shangzhou, Xi'an
Connecting lines: G4011 (Yangzhou-Liyang), G4012 (Liyang-Ningde), G4013 (Yangzhou-Leqing), G4015(Danfeng-Ningshan)

▶ G4012溧阳—宁德高速深渡服务区
Shendu Service Area along G4012 Liyang-Ningde Expressway

G42 上海—成都高速公路
Shanghai-Chengdu Expressway

▲ G42沪蓉高速重庆市巫山县境内
G42 Hurong Expressway in Wushan, Chongqing

名　　称：上海—成都高速公路（沪蓉高速）
编　　号：G42
主要控制点：上海、苏州、无锡、常州、南京、合肥、六安、麻城、武汉、孝感、荆门、宜昌、万州、垫江、广安、南充、遂宁、成都
联 络 线：4211(南京—芜湖)、G4212(合肥—安庆)、G4213(麻城—安康)、G4215(成都—遵义)、G4216(成都—丽江)、G4217(成都—昌都)、G4218(雅安—叶城)、G4219(曲水—乃东)、G4231(南京—九江)
并 行 线：G4221(上海—武汉)、G4222(和县—襄阳)、G4223(武汉—重庆)

Name: Shanghai-Chengdu Expressway (Hurong Expressway)
Number: G42
Main control points: Shanghai, Suzhou, Wuxi, Changzhou, Nanjing, Hefei, Lu'an, Macheng, Wuhan, Xiaogan, Jingmen, Yichang, Wanzhou, Dianjiang, Guang'an, Nanchong, Suining, Chengdu
Connecting lines: G4211 (Nanjing-Wuhu), G4212 (Hefei-Anqing), G4213 (Macheng- Ankang), G4215(Chengdu-Zunyi), G4216 (Chengdu-Lijiang), G4217 (Chengdu-Changdu), G4218 (Ya'an-Yecheng), G4219 (Qushui-Naidong), G4231 (Nanjing-Jiujiang)
Parallel lines: G4221 (Shanghai-Wuhan), G4222 (Hexian-Xiangyang), G4223 (Wuhan-Chongqing)

G42沪蓉高速是国家高速公路网 18 条东西横线中的第十横，是连接上海、江苏、安徽、湖北、重庆、四川的重要省际通道。G42沪蓉高速横贯我国长江经济带北部，是长江三角洲都市圈沿长江向中西部辐射的重要通道，对长江经济带北部的发展具有重要的支撑作用，对发展水路联运，带动长江经济带发展具有积极影响。

G42 Hurong Expressway is the 10th horizontal line of the 18 east-west horizontal lines in the national expressway network, and it is an important inter-provincial corridor connecting Shanghai, Jiangsu, Anhui, Hubei, Chongqing and Sichuan. G42 Hurong Expressway runs through the northern part of Yangtze River Economic Belt. It is an important corridor for the Yangtze River Delta metropolitan area to radiate to the central and western regions, and it is important for the development of northern part of the Yangtze River Economic Belt. It has a positive impact on improving the development of the Yangtze River Economic Belt.

▲ G42沪蓉高速新坪枢纽互通
Xinping Junction Interchange on G42 Hurong Expressway

◄ G42沪蓉高速湖北段
Hubei Section of G42 Hurong Expressway

EAST-WEST HORIZONTAL LINE 东西横线

▲ G42沪蓉高速神农溪大桥
Shennongxi Bridge on G42 Hurong Expressway

▲ G42沪蓉高速南京大胜关长江大桥
Nanjing Dashengguan Yangtze River Bridge on G42 Hurong Expressway

▲ G4211南京—芜湖高速千军服务区
Qianjun Service Area along G4211 Nanjing-Wuhu Expressway

上海—重庆高速公路
Shanghai-Chongqing Expressway

名　　称：上海—重庆高速公路（沪渝高速）
编　　号：G50
主要控制点：上海、湖州、宣城、芜湖、铜陵、安庆、黄梅、黄石、武汉、荆州、宜昌、恩施、忠县、垫江、重庆
联　络　线：G5011（芜湖—合肥）、G5012（恩施—广元）、G5013（重庆—成都）、G5015（武汉—岳阳）、G5016（宜昌—华容）
并　行　线：G5021（石柱—重庆）

Name: Shanghai-Chongqing Expressway (Huyu Expressway)
Number: G50
Main control points: Shanghai, Huzhou, Xuancheng, Wuhu, Tongling, Anqing, Huangmei, Huangshi, Wuhan, Jingzhou, Yichang, Enshi, Zhongxian, Dianjiang, Chongqing
Connecting lines: G5011 (Wuhu-Hefei), G5012 (Enshi-Guangyuan), G5013 (Chongqing-Chengdu), G5015 (Wuhan-Yueyang), G5016 (Yichang-Huarong)
Parallel line: G5021 (Shizhu-Chongqing)

◀ G50沪渝高速白果坝互通
Baiguoba Interchange on G50 Huyu Expressway

▲ G50沪渝高速利川互通
Lichuan Interchange on G50 Huyu Expressway

▲ G50沪渝高速马水河大桥
Mashui River Bridge on G50 Huyu Expressway

G50沪渝高速是国家高速公路网18条东西横线中的第十一横，是连接上海、江苏、浙江、安徽、湖北、重庆的重要省际通道。G50沪渝高速贯穿我国长江经济带南部，是长江三角洲都市圈沿江向中西部辐射的重要通道，对长江经济带南部的发展具有重要的支撑作用，对于加强长三角区域的经济活动往来具有重大意义，使中国东南沿海区域与内陆联系更加紧密。

G50 Huyu Expressway is the 11th horizontal line of the 18 east-west horizontal lines in the national expressway network, and it is an important inter-provincial corridor connecting Shanghai, Jiangsu, Zhejiang, Anhui, Hubei and Chongqing. G50 Huyu Expressway runs through the southern part of the Yangtze River Economic Belt. It is an important channel for the Yangtze River Delta metropolitan area to radiate to the central and western parts of China, and it is an important support for the development of the southern part of the Yangtze River Economic Belt. It is of great significance for the enhancement of the economic activities in the Yangtze River Delta.

▲ G5011芜湖—合肥高速试刀山隧道
Shidaoshan Tunnel on G5011 Wuhu-Hefei Expressway

▲ G50沪渝高速四渡河大桥
Sidu River Bridge on G50 Huyu Expressway

▲ G5011芜湖—合肥高速巢湖服务区
Chaohu Service Area along G5011 Wuhu-Hefei Expressway

杭州—瑞丽高速公路
Hangzhou-Ruili Expressway

名　　称：杭州—瑞丽高速公路（杭瑞高速）
编　　号：G56
主要控制点：杭州、黄山、景德镇、九江、咸宁、岳阳、常德、吉首、遵义、毕节、六盘水、曲靖、昆明、楚雄、大理、瑞丽（口岸）
联 络 线：G5611（大理—丽江）、G5612（大理—临沧）、G5613（保山—泸水）、G5615（天保—猴桥）、G5616（安乡—吉首）、G5617（临沧—勐海）、G5618（临沧—清水河）
并 行 线：G5621（昆明—大理）

Name: Hangzhou-Ruili Expressway (Hangrui Expressway)
Number: G56
Main control points: Hangzhou, Mount Huangshan, Jingdezhen, Jiujiang, Xianning, Yueyang, Changde, Jishou, Zunyi, Bijie, Liupanshui, Qujing, Kunming, Chuxiong, Dali, Ruili (checkpoint)
Connecting lines: G5611 (Dali-Lijiang), G5612 (Dali-Lincang), G5613 (Baoshan-Lushui), G5615 (Tianbao-Houqiao), G5616 (Anxiang-Jishou), G5617 (Lincang-Menghai), G5618 (Lincang-Qingshuihe)
Parallel line: G5621 (Kunming-Dali)

▲ G56杭瑞高速於潜枢纽
Yuqian Junction on G56 Hangrui Expressway

▲ G56杭瑞高速江西段
Jiangxi Section of G56 Hangrui Expressway

G56 杭瑞高速是国家高速公路网 18 条东西横线中的第十二横，是连接浙江、安徽、江西、湖北、湖南、贵州、云南的重要省际通道。G56 杭瑞高速是连接长三角和西南地区的重要高速公路通道，均衡了国土开发，改善了路网布局。同时，G56 杭瑞高速也是一条旅游热门线路，沿线旅游点密布，具有极高的带动旅游经济发展的价值。

G56 Hangrui Expressway is the 12th horizontal line of the 18 east-west horizontal lines in the national expressway network, and it is an important inter-provincial corridor connecting Zhejiang, Anhui, Jiangxi, Hubei, Hunan, Guizhou and Yunnan. G56 Hangrui Expressway is an important expressway corridor connecting the Yangtze River Delta and the southwest region, which balances the development of the land and improves the road network layout. G56 Hangrui Expressway is also a popular tourist route, with dense tourist spots along the route.

▲ G56杭瑞高速北盘江大桥
Beipan River Bridge on G56 Hangrui Expressway

▲ G56杭瑞高速普立特大桥
Puli Grand Bridge on G56 Hangrui Expressway

EAST-WEST HORIZONTAL LINE　　　　　　　　　　　　　　东　西　横　线

▲ G56杭瑞高速洞庭湖特大桥
Dongting Lake Grand Bridge on G56 Hangrui Expressway

G60 上海—昆明高速公路
Shanghai-Kunming Expressway

▲ G60沪昆高速嘉兴2号枢纽
No.2 Jiaxing Junction on G60 Hukun Expressway

EAST-WEST HORIZONTAL LINE　●────○　东 西 横 线

G60 沪昆高速是国家高速公路网 18 条东西横线中的第十三横，是连接上海、浙江、江西、湖南、贵州、云南的重要省际通道，有利于长江三角洲都市圈经济对华中、西南大中城市的辐射，对西南地区的经济发展起着重要的作用。同时，G60 沪昆高速具有较高的带动沿线旅游经济的能力，为沿途旅游业的发展创造了条件。

G60 Hukun Expressway is the 13th horizontal line of the 18 east-west horizontal lines in the national expressway network, and it is an important inter-provincial corridor connecting Shanghai, Zhejiang, Jiangxi, Hunan, Guizhou and Yunnan. It is beneficial for the radiation of the economy of the Yangtze River Delta metropolitan area to the large and medium-sized cities of Central and Southwest China. G60 Hukun Expressway also has a high ability to drive the tourism economy along the route, creating conditions for the development of tourism.

▲ G60沪昆高速江西段
Jiangxi Section of Hukun Expressway

名　　　称：上海—昆明高速公路（沪昆高速）
编　　　号：G60
主要控制点：上海、杭州、金华、衢州、上饶、鹰潭、南昌、宜春、长沙、邵阳、怀化、麻江、贵阳、安顺、曲靖、昆明
联　络　线：G6011（南昌—韶关）、G6012（曲靖—弥勒）
并　行　线：G6021（杭州—长沙）、G6022（醴陵—娄底）、G6023（南昌—凤凰）、G6025（洞口—三穗）

Name: Shanghai-Kunming Expressway (Hukun Expressway)
Number: G60
Main control points: Shanghai, Hangzhou, Jinhua, Quzhou, Shangrao, Yingtan, Nanchang, Yichun, Changsha, Shaoyang, Huaihua, Majiang, Guiyang, Anshun, Qujing, Kunming
Connecting lines: G6011 (Nanchang-Shaoguan), G6012 (Qujing-Mile)
Parallel lines: G6021 (Hangzhou-Changsha), G6022 (Liling-Loudi), G6023 (Nanchang-Fenghuang), G6025 (Dongkou-Sansui)

◀ G60沪昆高速贵州段
Guizhou Section of G60 Hukun Expressway

◀ G60沪昆高速红枫湖大桥
Hongfeng Lake Bridge on G60 Hukun Expressway

EAST-WEST HORIZONTAL LINE 　　東 西 横 線

▲ G60沪昆高速温泉服务区
Wenquan Service Area along G60 Hukun Expressway

中国高速公路　　　　　　　　　　　　　　　　　　　　　EXPRESSWAYS IN CHINA

G70 福州—银川高速公路
Fuzhou-Yinchuan Expressway

▼ G70福银高速襄阳互通
　Xiangyang Interchange on G70 Fuyin Expressway

名　　称：福州—银川高速公路（福银高速）
编　　号：G70
主要控制点：福州（长乐）、南平、南城、南昌、九江、黄梅、黄石、武汉、孝感、襄阳、十堰、商州、西安、平凉、中宁、银川
联 络 线：G7011（十堰—天水）、G7012（抚州—吉安）、G7013（沙县—南平）
并 行 线：G7021（宁德—武汉）

Name: Fuzhou-Yinchuan Expressway (Fuyin Expressway)
Number: G70
Main control points: Fuzhou (Changle), Nanping, Nancheng, Nanchang, Jiujiang, Huangmei, Huangshi, Wuhan, Xiaogan, Xiangyang, Shiyan, Shangzhou, Xi'an, Pingliang, Zhongning, Yinchuan
Connecting lines: G7011 (Shiyan-Tianshui), G7012 (Fuzhou-Ji'an), G7013 (Shaxian-Nanping)
Parallel line: G7021 (Ningde-Wuhan)

G70 福银高速是国家高速公路网 18 条东西横线中的第十四横，是连接福建、江西、湖北、陕西、甘肃、宁夏的重要省际通道，沟通了我国东南、华中与西北地区，是一条承东启西、贯穿南北的运输大动脉，打通了西北地区通往中原及东南沿海的高速通道，对于实施西部大开发战略，进一步促进东西部地区之间的交通和经济联系具有十分重大的意义。

G70 Fuyin Expressway is the 14th horizontal line of the 18 east-west horizontal lines in the national expressway network, and it is an important inter-provincial corridor connecting Fujian, Jiangxi, Hubei, Shaanxi, Gansu and Ningxia. It is a transportation artery, and it opens up the high-speed channel of the northwest region to the Central Plains and the southeast coast. It is important for the implementation of the Western Development Strategy, and further promoting the transportation and economic ties between the eastern and western regions.

▲ G70福银高速湖北段
Hubei Sefion of G70 Fuyin Expressway

中国高速公路　EXPRESSWAYS IN CHINA

▲ G70福银高速武当山服务区
Wudangshan Service Area along G70 Fuyin Expressway

▲ G70福银高速九江长江二桥
The Second Jiujiang Yangtze River Bridge on G70 Fuyin Expressway

▲ G7011十堰—天水高速公路西峡隧道
Xixia Tunnel on G7011 Shiyan-Tianshui Expressway

▲ G70福银高速临川服务区
Linchuan Service Area along G70 Fuyin Expressway

中国高速公路　　　　　　　　　　　　EXPRESSWAYS IN CHINA

G72 泉州—南宁高速公路
Quanzhou-Nanning Expressway

▲ G72泉南高速福建段
Fujian Section of G72 Quannan Expressway

名　　称：泉州—南宁高速公路（泉南高速）
编　　号：G72
主要控制点：泉州、永安、吉安、衡阳、永州、桂林、柳州、南宁
联 络 线：G7211（南宁—友谊关）、G7212（柳州—北海）
并 行 线：G7221（衡阳—南宁）

Name: Quanzhou-Nanning Expressway (Quannan Expressway)
Number: G72
Main control points: Quanzhou, Yong'an, Ji'an, Hengyang, Yongzhou, Guilin, Liuzhou, Nanning
Connecting lines: G7211 (Nanning - Youyiguan), G7212 (Liuzhou - Beihai)
Parallel line: G7221 (Hengyang - Nanning)

EAST-WEST HORIZONTAL LINE 东 西 横 线

▲ G72泉南高速与S40梧硕高速互通
Interchange between G72 Quannan Expressway and S40 Wushuo Expressway

G72 泉南高速是国家高速公路网 18 条东西横线中的第十五横，连接华东东南沿海、华中和华南西部地区，有利于改善路网布局，是连接中国南部地区与东南亚地区的重要经济通道。

G72 Quannan Expressway is the 15th horizontal line of the 18 east-west horizontal lines in the national expressway network, connecting the southeast coast of East China, Central China and the western part of South China. It is beneficial for the improvement of the layout of the road network, and it is an important economic corridor between the southern part of China and the Southeast Asia.

▶ G72泉南高速三阳隧道
Sanyang Tunnel on G72 Quannan Expressway

G76 厦门—成都高速公路
Xiamen-Chengdu Expressway

▲ G76厦蓉高速赣县东互通
Ganxian East Interchange on G76 Xiarong Expressway

▲ G76厦蓉高速会昌贡水大桥
Huichang Gongshui Bridge on G76 Xiarong Expressway

名　　称：厦门—成都高速公路（厦蓉高速）
编　　号：G76
主要控制点：厦门、漳州、龙岩、瑞金、赣州、郴州、桂林、都匀、贵阳、毕节、泸州、隆昌、内江、成都
联 络 线：G7611（都匀—香格里拉）、G7612（纳雍—兴义）

Name: Xiamen-Chengdu Expressway (Xiarong Expressway)
Number: G76
Main control points: Xiamen, Zhangzhou, Longyan, Ruijin, Ganzhou, Chenzhou, Guilin, Duyun, Guiyang, Bijie, Luzhou, Longchang, Neijiang, Chengdu
Connecting lines: G7611 (Duyun – Shangri-La), G7612 (Nayong – Xingyi)

G76 厦蓉高速是国家高速公路网 18 条东西横线中的第十六横，是连接福建、江西、湖南、广西、贵州、四川的重要省际通道。G76 厦蓉高速是我国西南腹地通往东南沿海地区的重要出海通道，加强了我国西部地区与东南沿海地区的联系，有利于改善路网布局和国土均衡开发，是西南地区连接东部的重要经济通道。

◀ G76厦蓉高速泸州长江二桥
The Second Luzhou Yangtze River Bridge on G76 Xiarong Expressway

▲ G7611都匀—香格里拉高速六盘水至六枝段
Liupanshui–Liuzhi Section of G7611 Duyun – Shangri-La Expressway

EAST-WEST HORIZONTAL LINE　　　　　东 西 横 线

▲ G76厦蓉高速飘勺洞大桥
Piaoshaodong Bridge on G76 Xiarong Expressway

▲ G76厦蓉高速会昌服务区
Huichang Service Area along G76 Xiarong Expressway

G76 Xiarong Expressway is the 16th horizontal line of the 18 east-west horizontal lines in the national expressway network, and it is an important inter-provincial corridor connecting Fujian, Jiangxi, Hunan, Guangxi, Guizhou and Sichuan. G76 Xiarong Expressway is an important sea passage from the southwest hinterland of China to the southeast coastal area, which strengthens the connection between the western region of China and the southeast coastal area. It is beneficial for the improvement of the layout of the road network and for balancing the development of land.

G78 汕头—昆明高速公路
Shantou-Kunming Expressway

▲ G78汕昆高速百色市互通
Baise City Interchange on G78 Shankun Expressway

EAST-WEST HORIZONTAL LINE 东西横线

▲ G78汕昆高速广西段
Guangxi Section of G78 Shankun Expressway

名　　称：汕头—昆明高速公路（汕昆高速）
编　　号：G78
主要控制点：汕头、梅州、韶关、贺州、柳州、河池、兴义、石林、昆明

Name: Shantou-Kunming Expressway (Shankun Expressway)
Number: G78
Main control points: Shantou, Meizhou, Shaoguan, Hezhou, Liuzhou, Hechi, Xingyi, Shilin, Kunming

G78汕昆高速是国家高速公路网18条东西横线中的第十七横，是连接广东、广西、贵州、云南的重要省际通道。G78汕昆高速是西南地区连接东部的重要经济通道，有利于改善路网布局和交通分布。

G78 Shankun Expressway is the 17th horizontal line of the 18 east-west horizontal lines in the national expressway network, and it is an important inter-provincial corridor connecting Guangdong, Guangxi, Guizhou and Yunnan. G78 Shankun Expressway is an important economic corridor connecting the southwest region to the east, which is beneficial for the improvement of the layout of the road network and the distribution of traffic.

▲ G78汕昆高速马岭河大桥
Maling River Bridge on G78 Shankun Expressway

▲ G78汕昆高速大桂山隧道
Daguishan Tunnel on G78 Shankun Expressway

▲ G78汕昆高速者告河特大桥
Zhegao River Grand Bridge on G78 Shankun Expressway

EAST-WEST HORIZONTAL LINE 东 西 横 线

▲ G78汕昆高速旧州服务区
Jiuzhou Service Area along G78 Shankun Expressway

中国高速公路 EXPRESSWAYS IN CHINA

 # G80 广州—昆明高速公路
Guangzhou–Kunming Expressway

▲ G80广昆高速与G8011开远—河口高速互通
Interchange between G80 Guangkun Expressway and G8011 Kaiyuan–Hekou Expressway

EAST-WEST HORIZONTAL LINE 东西横线

▲ G8011开远—河口高速南盘江特大桥
Nanpan River Grand Bridge on G8011 Kaiyuan-Hekou Expressway

G80 广昆高速是国家高速公路网 18 条东西横线中的第十八横，是连接广东、广西、云南的重要省际通道，连接华南地区与西南地区，是西南地区另一条重要的出海通道。

G80 Guangkun Expressway is the 18th horizontal line of the 18 east-west horizontal lines in the national expressway network, and it is an important inter-provincial corridor connecting Guangdong, Guangxi and Yunnan. It connects South and Southwest China, and is another important sea access in Southwest China.

名　　称：广州—昆明高速公路（广昆高速）
编　　号：G80
主要控制点：广州、肇庆、梧州、玉林、南宁、百色、富宁、开远、石林、昆明
联 络 线：G8011（开远—河口）、G8012（弥勒—楚雄）、G8013（砚山—文山）

Name: Guangzhou-Kunming Expressway (Guangkun Expressway)
Number: G80
Main control points: Guangzhou, Zhaoqing, Wuzhou, Yulin, Nanning, Baise, Funing, Kaiyuan, Shilin, Kunming
Connecting lines: G8011 (Kaiyuan-Hekou), G8012 (Mile-Chuxiong), G8013 (Yanshan-Wenshan)

▲ G80广昆高速朋普服务区
Pengpu Service Area along G80 Guangkun Expressway

地区环线
REGIONAL RING ROAD

G91　G92　G93　G94
G95　G98

中国高速公路
EXPRESSWAYS IN CHINA

G91 辽中地区环线高速公路
Ring Expressway in the Central Liaoning Region

▲ G91辽中地区环线高速辽宁段
Liaoning Section of G91 Ring Expressway in the Central Liaoning Region

名　　　称：辽中地区环线高速公路
编　　　号：G91
主要控制点：铁岭、抚顺、本溪、辽阳、辽中、新民、铁岭
联　络　线：G9111（本溪—集安）

Name: Ring Expressway in the Central Liaoning Region
Number: G91
Main control points: Tieling, Fushun, Benxi, Liaoyang, Liaozhong, Xinmin, Tieling
Connecting line: G9111 (Benxi-Ji'an)

　　G91辽中地区环线高速公路是国家高速公路网6条地区环线中的第一环，连接辽宁中部的沈阳周边城市，同时连接着沈海、京哈等国家干线高速和数条联络线，是这一地区城市群之间的重要通道，也是辽宁中部地区重要的经济环线。

G91 Ring Expressway in the central Liaoning region is the first ring road of the six regional ring roads in the national expressway network, connecting the cities around Shenyang in central Liaoning, as well as the national trunk expressways such as Shenhai, Jingha, and several connecting lines. It is an important channel between the city clusters of the region, and is also an important economic ring road in the central region of Liaoning.

REGIONAL RING ROAD 地 区 环 线

▲ G91辽中地区环线高速与G1京哈高速互通
Interchange between G91 Ring Expressway in the Central Liaoning Region and G1 Jingha Expressway

G92 杭州湾地区环线高速公路
Ring Expressway in the Hangzhou Bay Area

名　　称：杭州湾地区环线高速公路
编　　号：G92
主要控制点：上海、杭州、宁波、上海
联 络 线：G9211（宁波—舟山）
并 行 线：G9221（杭州—宁波）

Name: Ring Expressway in the Hangzhou Bay Area
Number: G92
Main control points: Shanghai, Hangzhou, Ningbo, Shanghai
Connecting line: G9211 (Ningbo-Zhoushan)
Parallel line: G9221 (Hangzhou-Ningbo)

▲ G92杭州湾地区环线高速宁波东互通
Ningbo East Interchange on G92 Ring Expressway in the Hangzhou Bay Area

REGIONAL RING ROAD 地 区 环 线

G92 杭州湾地区环线高速公路是国家高速公路网6条地区环线中的第二环,连接杭州湾周边城市,是这一地区的重要经济通道。G92 杭州湾地区环线高速公路连接沪陕、沪蓉、沪渝、京沪、长深、杭瑞等六条国家干线高速公路,并与沈海、沪昆高速公路重合,推动了整个长江三角洲地区城市之间的交流。

G92 Ring Expressway in the Hangzhou Bay area is the second ring road of the six regional ring roads in the national expressway network, connecting the cities around Hangzhou Bay, and it is an important economic corridor in the region. G92 Ring Expressway in the Hangzhou Bay area connects six national trunk expressways, including Hushan, Hurong, Huyu, Jinghu, Changshen and Hangrui, and overlaps with Shenhai and Hukun expressways, promoting exchanges between cities in the entire Yangtze River Delta region.

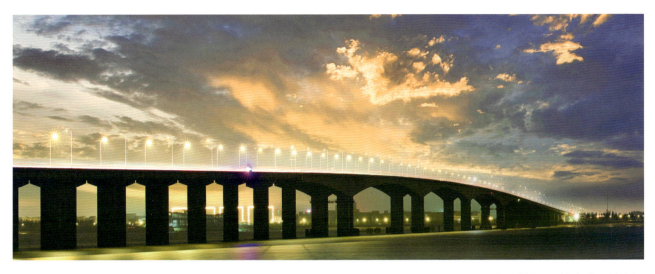

▲ G92杭州湾地区环线高速下沙大桥
Xiasha Bridge on G92 Ring Expressway in the Hangzhou Bay Area

▲ G9211宁波—舟山高速舟山服务区
Zhoushan Service Area along G9211 Ningbo-Zhoushan Expressway

▲ G9211宁波—舟山高速浙江段
Zhejiang Section of G9211 Ningbo-Zhoushan Expressway

中国高速公路　　EXPRESSWAYS IN CHINA

成渝地区环线高速公路
Ring Expressway in the Chengdu-Chongqing Region

名　　　称：成渝地区环线高速公路
编　　　号：G93
主要控制点：成都、绵阳、遂宁、重庆、合江、泸州、宜宾、乐山、雅安、成都

Name: Ring Expressway in the Chengdu-Chongqing Region
Number: G93
Main control points: Chengdu, Mianyang, Suining, Chongqing, Hejiang, Luzhou, Yibin, Leshan, Ya'an, Chengdu

▲ G93成渝地区环线高速龙凤古镇收费站
Longfeng Town Toll Station on G93 Ring Expressway in the Chengdu-Chongqing Region

　　G93 成渝地区环线高速公路是国家高速公路网 6 条地区环线中的第三环，连接四川中部和重庆，是这一地区城市之间的重要通道。G93 成渝地区环线高速公路连接沪蓉、沪渝、包茂、兰海、厦蓉、渝昆等国家干线高速公路，带动了沿线地区的经济发展。

G93 Ring Expressway in the Chengdu-Chongqing region is the third ring road of the six regional ring roads in the national expressway network, connecting central Sichuan and Chongqing, and it is an important channel between the cities in this region. G93 Ring Expressway in the Chengdu-Chongqing region connects the national trunk expressways including Hurong, Huyu, Baomao, Lanhai, Xiarong and Yukun, and promotes the economic development of the areas along the route.

REGIONAL RING ROAD ● ○ 地 区 环 线

▲ G93成渝地区环线高速南溪长江大桥
Nanxi Yangtze River Bridge on G93 Ring Expressway in the Chengdu-Chongqing Region

▲ G93成渝地区环线高速象鼻互通
Xiangbi Interchange on G93 Ring Expressway in the Chengdu-Chongqing Region

G94 珠江三角洲地区环线高速公路
Ring Expressway in the Pearl River Delta Region

G94 珠江三角洲地区环线高速公路是国家高速公路网 6 条地区环线中的第四环，是珠江三角洲地区城市之间的重要经济通道，有利于加强香港、澳门与珠江三角洲地区的沟通，是粤港澳大湾区重要的公路基础设施之一。G94 珠江三角洲地区环线高速公路连接沈海、长深、济广、大广、京港澳、二广和广昆 7 条国家干线高速公路，加快了沿线地区的经济发展。

G94 Ring Expressway in the Pearl River Delta region is the fourth ring road of the six regional ring roads in the national expressway network, and it is an important economic corridor between cities in the region. It is beneficial for strengthening the communication between Hong Kong, Macao and the Pearl River Delta region, and it is one of the important highway infrastructures in the Guangdong-Hong Kong-Macao Greater Bay Area. G94 Ring Expressway in the Pearl River Delta region connects seven national trunk expressways including Shenhai, Changshen, Jiguang, Daguang, Jinggang'ao, Erguang and Guangkun, and it accelerates the economic development of the areas along the route.

▼ G94珠江三角洲地区环线高速港珠澳大桥
Hong Kong-Zhuhai-Macao Bridge on G94 Ring Expressway in the Pearl River Delta Region

REGIONAL RING ROAD　　　　　　　　　　　　　　　　　　　地　区　环　线

▲ G94珠江三角洲地区环线高速与珠海南湾北路互通
Interchange between G94 Ring Expressway in the Pearl River Delta Region and Nanwan North Road in Zhuhai

▲ G94珠江三角洲地区环线高速清湖互通
Qinghu Interchange on G94 Ring Expressway in the Pearl River Delta Region

名　　　称：珠江三角洲地区环线高速公路
编　　　号：G94
主要控制点：深圳、香港（口岸）、澳门（口岸）、珠海、中山、江门、佛山、
　　　　　　花都、增城、东莞、深圳
联　络　线：G9411（东莞—佛山）

Name: Ring Expressway in the Pearl River Delta Region
Number: G94
Main control points: Shenzhen, Hong Kong (checkpoint), Macao (checkpoint), Zhuhai, Zhongshan, Jiangmen, Foshan, Huadu, Zengcheng, Dongguan, Shenzhen
Connecting line: G9411 (Dongguan–Foshan)

▶ G94珠江三角洲地区环线高速港珠澳大桥口岸人工岛和收费站
Artificial Island and Toll Station of Hong Kong–Zhuhai–Macao Bridge Checkpoint on G94 Ring Expressway in the Pearl River Delta Region

143

G95 首都地区环线高速公路
Ring Expressway in the Capital Region

▲ G95首都地区环线高速河北张家口段
Hebei Zhangjiakou Section of G95 Ring Expressway in the Capital Region

REGIONAL RING ROAD 地 区 环 线

名　　　称：首都地区环线高速公路
编　　　号：G95
主要控制点：承德、遵化、玉田、蓟州、宝坻、宁河、武清、廊坊、固安、涿州、涿鹿、张家口、崇礼、沽源、丰宁、承德
联　络　线：G9511（涞水—涞源）

Name: Ring Expressway in the Capital Region
Number: G95
Main control points: Chengde, Zunhua, Yutian, Jizhou, Baodi, Ninghe, Wuqing, Langfang, Gu'an, Zhuozhou, Zhuolu, Zhangjiakou, Chongli, Guyuan, Fengning, Chengde
Connecting lines: G9511 (Laishui-Laiyuan)

▲ G95首都地区环线高速河北承德段
Hebei Chengde Section of G95 Ring Expressway in the Capital Region

▼ G95首都地区环线高速北运河高架桥
Beiyunhe Viaduct on G95 Ring Expressway in the Capital Region

G95 首都地区环线高速公路是国家高速公路网 6 条地区环线中的第五环，对促进京津冀地区经济发展具有十分重要的意义。

G95 Ring Expressway in the capital region is the fifth ring road of the six regional ring roads in the national expressway network. It is of great significance to promote the economic development of Beijing-Tianjin-Hebei region.

G98 海南地区环线高速公路
Ring Expressway in Hainan

▼ G98海南地区环线高速牛岭隧道
Niuling Tunnel on G98 Ring Expressway in Hainan

REGIONAL RING ROAD 地区环线

G98 海南地区环线高速公路是国家高速公路网 6 条地区环线中的第六环，是连接海南岛沿海城市的环岛高速公路，通过琼州海峡连接沈海和兰海两条国家干线高速公路，对海南地区的经济及旅游发展起到促进作用。

G98 Ring Expressway in Hainan is the sixth ring road of the six regional ring roads in the national expressway network, and it is a ring expressway connecting the coastal cities of Hainan Island. It connects two national trunk expressways including Shenhai and Lanhai through the Qiongzhou Strait, and plays a role in promoting the economic and tourism development in Hainan.

◀ G98海南地区环线高速迎宾互通
Yingbin Interchange on G98 Ring Expressway in Hainan

名　　称：海南地区环线高速公路
编　　号：G98
主要控制点：海口、琼海、三亚、东方、海口
联　络　线：G9811（海口—乐东）、G9812（海口—琼海）、G9813（万宁—洋浦）

Name: Ring Expressway in Hainan
Number: G98
Main control points: Haikou, Qionghai, Sanya, Dongfang, Haikou
Connecting lines: G9811 (Haikou-Ledong), G9812 (Haikou-Qionghai), G9813 (Wanning-Yangpu)

▶ G9812海口—琼海高速冯家湾服务区
Fengjiawan Service Area along G9812 Haikou–Qionghai Expressway

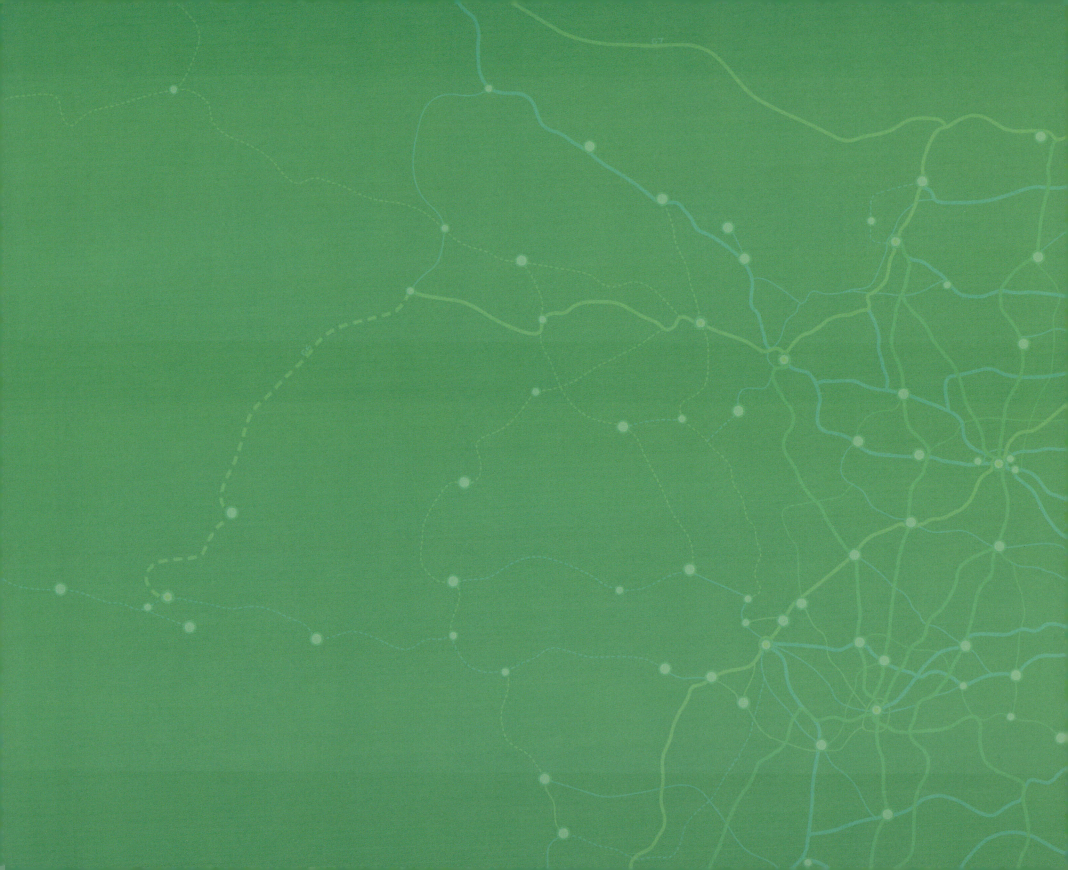

都市圈环线
RING ROAD IN METROPOLITAN CIRCLE

中国高速公路
EXPRESSWAYS IN CHINA

都市圈环线高速公路（12条）
Twelve Ring Expressways in Metropolitan Circles

名称 Name	编号 Number	主要控制点 Main control points
哈尔滨都市圈环线高速公路 Ring Expressway in Harbin Metropolitan Circle	G9901	双城、松北、呼兰、阿城、双城 Shuangcheng, Songbei, Hulan, Acheng, and Shuangcheng
长春都市圈环线高速公路 Ring Expressway in Changchun Metropolitan Circle	G9902	德惠、九台、双阳、伊通、公主岭、农安、德惠 Dehui, Jiutai, Shuangyang, Yitong, Gongzhuling, Nong'an, and Dehui
杭州都市圈环线高速公路 Ring Expressway in Hangzhou Metropolitan Circle	G9903	德清、桐乡、海宁、绍兴、诸暨、富阳、德清 Deqing, Tongxiang, Haining, Shaoxing, Zhuji, Fuyang, and Deqing
南京都市圈环线高速公路 Ring Expressway in Nanjing Metropolitan Circle	G9904	来安、天长、仪征、句容、南京、全椒、滁州、来安 Lai'an, Tianchang, Yizheng, Jurong, Nanjing, Quanjiao, Chuzhou, and Lai'an
郑州都市圈环线高速公路 Ring Expressway in Zhengzhou Metropolitan Circle	G9905	荥阳、中牟、尉氏、新郑、新密、荥阳 Xingyang, Zhongmou, Weishi, Xinzheng, Xinmi, and Xingyang
武汉都市圈环线高速公路 Ring Expressway in Wuhan Metropolitan Circle	G9906	华容、梁子湖、汉南、汉川、孝感、新洲、华容 Huarong, Liangzihu, Hannan, Hanchuan, Xiaogan, Xinzhou, and Huarong
长株潭都市圈环线高速公路 Ring Expressway in Changsha-Zhuzhou-Xiangtan Metropolitan Circle	G9907	宁乡、浏阳、醴陵、湘乡、韶山、宁乡 Ningxiang, Liuyang, Liling, Xiangxiang, Shaoshan, and Ningxiang
西安都市圈环线高速公路 Ring Expressway in Xi'an Metropolitan Circle	G9908	蓝田、鄠邑、周至、武功、乾县、富平、渭南、蓝田 Lantian, Huyi, Zhouzhi, Wugong, Qianxian, Fuping, Weinan, and Lantian
重庆都市圈环线高速公路 Ring Expressway in Chongqing Metropolitan Circle	G9909	永川、铜梁、合川、长寿、涪陵、南川、綦江、永川 Yongchuan, Tongliang, Hechuan, Changshou, Fuling, Nanchuan, Qijiang, and Yongchuan
成都都市圈环线高速公路 Ring Expressway in Chengdu Metropolitan Circle	G9910	都江堰、什邡、德阳、中江、彭山、蒲江、都江堰 Dujiangyan, Shifang, Deyang, Zhongjiang, Pengshan, Pujiang, and Dujiangyan
济南都市圈环线高速公路 Ring Expressway in Jinan Metropolitan Circle	G9911	长清、齐河、禹城、临邑、济阳、章丘、长清 Changqing, Qihe, Yucheng, Linyi, Jiyang, Zhangqiu, and Changqing
合肥都市圈环线高速公路 Ring Expressway in Hefei Metropolitan Circle	G9912	肥东、巢湖、肥西、肥东 Feidong, Chaohu, Feixi, and Feidong

RING ROAD IN METROPOLITAN CIRCLE 　都 市 圈 环 线

▲ G9903杭州都市圈环线高速
G9903 Ring Expressway in Hangzhou Metropolitan Circle

▲ G9904南京都市圈环线高速
G9904 Ring Expressway in Nanjing Metropolitan Circle

RING ROAD IN METROPOLITAN CIRCLE 都 市 圈 环 线

▲ G9909重庆都市圈环线高速
G9909 Ring Expressway in Chongqing Metropolitan Circle

▲ G9910成都都市圈环线高速
G9910 Ring Expressway in Chengdu Metropolitan Circle

RING ROAD IN METROPOLITAN CIRCLE　　都 市 圈 环 线

▲ G9912合肥都市圈环线高速
G9912 Ring Expressway in Hefei Metropolitan Circle

城市绕城环线

URBAN RING ROAD

中国高速公路

EXPRESSWAYS IN CHINA

城市绕城环线高速公路（30条）
Thirty Urban Ring Expressways

名称 Name	编号 Number	名称 Name	编号 Number
长沙市绕城高速公路 Changsha Ring Expressway	G0401	石家庄市绕城高速公路 Shijiazhuang Ring Expressway	G2002
西宁市绕城高速公路 Xining Ring Expressway	G0601	太原市绕城高速公路 Taiyuan Ring Expressway	G2003
沈阳市绕城高速公路 Shenyang Ring Expressway	G1501	银川市绕城高速公路 Yinchuan Ring Expressway	G2004
上海市绕城高速公路 Shanghai Ring Expressway	G1503	兰州市绕城高速公路 Lanzhou Ring Expressway	G2201
宁波市绕城高速公路 Ningbo Ring Expressway	G1504	郑州市绕城高速公路 Zhengzhou Ring Expressway	G3001
福州市绕城高速公路 Fuzhou Ring Expressway	G1505	西安市绕城高速公路 Xi'an Ring Expressway	G3002
广州市绕城高速公路 Guangzhou Ring Expressway	G1508	乌鲁木齐市绕城高速公路 Urumqi Ring Expressway	G3003
长春市绕城高速公路 Changchun Ring Expressway	G2501	合肥市绕城高速公路 Hefei Ring Expressway	G4001
天津市绕城高速公路 Tianjin Ring Expressway	G2502	武汉市绕城高速公路 Wuhan Ring Expressway	G4201
南京市绕城高速公路 Nanjing Ring Expressway	G2503	成都市绕城高速公路 Chengdu Ring Expressway	G4202
杭州市绕城高速公路 Hangzhou Ring Expressway	G2504	重庆市绕城高速公路 Chongqing Ring Expressway	G5001
北京市绕城高速公路 Beijing Ring Expressway	G4501	昆明市绕城高速公路 Kunming Ring Expressway	G5601
呼和浩特市绕城高速公路 Hohhot Ring Expressway	G5901	南昌市绕城高速公路 Nanchang Ring Expressway	G6001
哈尔滨市绕城高速公路 Harbin Ring Expressway	G1001	贵阳市绕城高速公路 Guiyang Ring Expressway	G6002
济南市绕城高速公路 Jinan Ring Expressway	G2001	南宁市绕城高速公路 Nanning Ring Expressway	G7201

URBAN RING ROAD 城 市 绕 城 环 线

▲ G0401长沙市绕城高速湘江特大桥
Xiangjiang River Grand Bridge on G0401 Changsha Ring Expressway

▲ G1501沈阳市绕城高速东陵段
Dongling Section of G1501 Shenyang Ring Expressway

▲ G1503上海市绕城高速与S26沪常高速互通
Interchange between G1503 Shanghai Ring Expressway and S26 Huchang Expressway

▲ G1504宁波市绕城高速蛟川枢纽
Jiaochuan Junction on G1504 Ningbo Ring Expressway

▲ G1505福州市绕城高速长门特大桥
Changmen Grand Bridge on G1505 Fuzhou Ring Expressway

▲ G2001济南市绕城高速港沟立交
Ganggou Interchange on G2001 Jinan Ring Expressway

▲ G1508广州市绕城高速顺德东立交
Shunde East Interchange on G1508 Guangzhou Ring Expressway

▲ G2002石家庄市绕城高速与G4京港澳高速互通
　Interchange between G2002 Shijiazhuang Ring Expressway and G4 Jinggang'ao Expressway

▲ G2003太原市绕城高速汾河特大桥
Fenhe River Grand Bridge on G2003 Taiyuan Ring Expressway

▲ G2503南京市绕城高速东山枢纽
Dongshan Junction on G2503 Nanjing Ring Expressway

▲ G2004银川市绕城高速阅海大桥
Yuehai Bridge on G2004 Yinchuan Ring Expressway

▲ G2504杭州市绕城高速黄鹤山隧道
Huangheshan Tunnel on G2504 Hangzhou Ring Expressway

URBAN RING ROAD　　　　　　　　　城 市 绕 城 环 线

▲ G3002西安绕城高速曲江互通
Qujiang Interchange on G3002 Xi'an Ring Expressway

▲ G4001合肥市绕城高速陇西互通
Longxi Interchange on G4001 Hefei Ring Expressway

URBAN RING ROAD　　　城市绕城环线

▲ G4201武汉市绕城高速青山长江大桥
Qingshan Yangtze River Bridge on G4201 Wuhan Ring Expressway

▲ G4202成都市绕城高速狮子互通
Shizi Interchange on G4202 Chengdu Ring Expressway

▲ G4202成都市绕城高速与G317国道互通
Interchange between G4202 Chengdu Ring Expressway and G317 National Highway

▲ G4501北京市绕城高速百葛互通
Baige Interchange on G4501 Beijing Ring Expressway

▲ G5001重庆市绕城高速水土嘉陵江大桥
Shuitu Jialing River Bridge on G5001 Chongqing Ring Expressway

▲ G5601昆明市绕城高速与S27呈元高速互通
Interchange between G5601 Kunming Ring Expressway and S27 Chengyuan Expressway

URBAN RING ROAD 城市绕城环线

▲ G7201南宁市绕城高速安吉互通
Anji Interchange on G7201 Nanning Ring Expressway

▲ G6002贵阳市绕城高速与G60沪昆高速互通
Interchange between G6002 Guiyang Ring Expressway and G60 Hukun Expressway

后 记

为展示奋力加快建设交通强国，努力当好中国式现代化开路先锋的成就，让国内外更好地了解中国交通发展，我们策划出版了"中国交通名片丛书"。其中，《中国高速公路》分册得到了交通运输部公路局的大力支持。

本书编写力求科学严谨、求真务实。交通运输部规划研究院等单位对本书内容进行了细致审核并提出了很多建设性意见。

编写出版过程中，北京、天津、山西、内蒙古、江苏、浙江、安徽、福建、江西、河南、湖北、广东、海南、陕西、青海、宁夏、新疆等地交通运输主管部门，以及湖北省交通投资集团有限公司、福建省高速公路集团有限公司等单位提出了很多好的意见和建议。

人民交通出版社对本书的出版非常重视，社领导舒驰、刘韬、陈志敏多次提出宝贵意见，吴有铭、刘永超、黎小东、丁遥、师静圆、侯蓓蓓、刘彤等同志为本书编辑做了大量工作。

经过 30 多年的跨越式发展，中国高速公路取得了举世瞩目的发展成就，一项项技术难关被攻克、一个个"超级工程"陆续问世，高速公路已成为一张亮丽的"中国名片"。受编写资料和篇幅所限，本书难免挂一漏万，存在不足之处，欢迎广大读者提出宝贵意见、建议，便于我们及时修订完善，以期更好地宣传好、展示好这张"中国名片"！

编者

2024 年 9 月

EPILOGUE

In order to show the achievements of building China into a country with great transport strength and being the trailblazer in China's modernization drive, and enable domestic and international readers to better understand China's transport development, we have planned and published the "Card Book Series: Transport in China". Among them, the volume titled "Expressways in China" has received strong support from the Highway Department of the Ministry of Transport.

When compiling this book, we strive to be scientifically rigorous, realistic and pragmatic. Units such as the Transport Planning and Research Institute of the Ministry of Transport conducted detailed review of the content and offered many constructive suggestions.

During the compilation and publication process, the transport authorities in Beijing, Tianjin, Shanxi, Inner Mongolia, Jiangsu, Zhejiang, Anhui, Fujian, Jiangxi, Henan, Hubei, Guangdong, Hainan, Shaanxi, Qinghai, Ningxia, and Xinjiang, as well as the Hubei Communications Investment Group Co., Ltd. and Fujian Expressway Group Co., Ltd., and other units, provided many valuable opinions and suggestions.

China Communications Press attaches great importance to the publication of this book, and its management Shu Chi, Liu Tao, and Chen Zhimin have offered valuable opinions and suggestions on multiple occasions. Wu Youming, Liu Yongchao, Li Xiaodong, Ding Yao, Shi Jingyuan, Hou Beibei, Liu Tong and other colleagues did a lot of work for the editing of this book.

After more than 30 years of leapfrog development, China has made remarkable achievements in expressway development. Technical difficulties have been overcome, and "super works" have been launched successively one after another. Expressway has become a brilliant "business card of China". Due to the limitation of compilation materials and space, there are inevitably some deficiencies in this book. We welcome readers to put forward valuable opinions and suggestions so that we can revise and improve it in time and better display this "business card of China".

Editors
September 2024

图书在版编目（CIP）数据

中国高速公路：汉文、英文 /《中国高速公路》编写组编 . — 北京：人民交通出版社股份有限公司，2024. 10. — ISBN 978-7-114-19726-0

Ⅰ. U412.36

中国国家版本馆 CIP 数据核字第 20249RA690 号

本书由人民交通出版社独家出版发行。未经著作权人书面许可，本书图片及文字任何部分，不得以任何方式和手段进行复制、转载或刊登。版权所有，侵权必究。

Copyright © 2024

All rights reserved. No part of this publication may be reproduced, stored in a retrieval system, or transmitted in any form or by any means, electronic, mechanical, photocopying, recording or otherwise, without the prior written permission of the copyright holder. Printed in China.

Zhongguo Gaosu Gonglu

书　　　名：	中国高速公路
著 作 者：	《中国高速公路》编写组
责任编辑：	吴有铭　刘永超　黎小东　丁　遥
责任校对：	赵媛媛　魏佳宁
责任印制：	张　凯
出版发行：	人民交通出版社
地　　　址：	（100011）北京市朝阳区安定门外外馆斜街3号
网　　　址：	http：//www.ccpcl.com.cn
销售电话：	（010）85285857
总 经 销：	人民交通出版社发行部
经　　　销：	各地新华书店
印　　　刷：	北京雅昌艺术印刷有限公司
开　　　本：	965×635　1/8
印　　　张：	23.5
字　　　数：	234千
版　　　次：	2024年10月　第1版
印　　　次：	2024年10月　第1次印刷
书　　　号：	ISBN 978-7-114-19726-0
定　　　价：	368.00元

（有印刷、装订质量问题的图书，由本社负责调换）